women will save the world

women will
save the world

By Caroline A. Shearer
Edited by Sarah Hackley

**Absolute Love
Publishing**

Absolute Love Publishing

Women Will Save the World

Published by
Absolute Love Publishing
USA

Copyright © Caroline A. Shearer
Cover design by Meaghan Thiede
Cover headshot by Prabhakar Gopalan

ISBN-13: 978-0-9833017-2-1
United States of America

For

Mary Anne and Kimberly

Alivia, Caroline, Sarah, and Catie

"The world will be saved by the Western woman."
– His Holiness, the Dalai Lama
Vancouver Peace Summit 2009

contents

🌸 Nurturing

⚓ Strength

🦋 Trailblazing

👁 Wisdom

introduction

A few years ago, I sat at a tiny table in the middle of Whole Foods and announced to my editor, "I came across a quote from the Dalai Lama, and I want to write a book about it."

I can picture myself even now, talking rapidly, almost popping out of myself with excitement, with loads of animated hand gestures and a big smile. "It's incredibly profound, and I can't get it out of my head!" I said. Then, for effect, I moved my hand across the sky like it was lighting up a billboard: "The world will be saved by the western woman."

As an intuitive person, the prophetic nature of the statement intrigues me even to this day. It is simple, profound, and staggering to consider. Is it really our destiny to save humanity? Are we at a point and place in time when, being the best and most complete version of ourselves, we will harness our feminine nature and use it for the good of all? What would saving the world look like? Would it be dramatic in superhero fashion, or would it be a quiet, collective impact that steadily grew more and more powerful as we each stepped fully into the beauty of our womanhood?

Perhaps asking these questions is the beginning.

As a writer, I have the luxury of exploring my trains of thought and personal questions in a very public way, and my desire to create a book such as this is perhaps the expression of a larger thought process at work. The quote was a trigger, but the idea probably had long wanted to hop out of my head and onto the pages of a book.

I am of the generation that has always experienced equality, or at least I certainly have in my life. I never had to "fight" those battles. If you would have asked me at eight or ten or twelve years old, I would have said, "Of course, we're equal!" It was never a question for me. I excelled at some things, received a fair share of attention, had opportunities, made opportunities, and generally appreciated my position as a female.

Somewhere in my tween years, I remember saying, "I am so glad I am a girl!"

To me, being a boy meant difficult things – like asking girls out – and I was way too much of a chicken for that! At the time, of course, I did not fully grasp the complexity of being a woman, but I think the thread of understanding that it was something truly wonderful already was ingrained.

For about ten minutes in high school, I bought into a pop psychology phase that men and women were virtually the same. I'm sure I vowed to give my future daughters trucks to play with and my future sons, dolls. When my mother tried to express her observations that there were distinct differences between boys and girls, I probably rolled my eyes at her "old-fashioned" wisdom. Yes, I pretty much knew it all.

In college, my favorite classes were ones in which I was able to study women writers and the psychology of women. How I loved them! But, they tended to be about the dark side of being a woman – overwhelming emotional distress that resulted in dire consequences, adolescent angst that caused lifelong damage, in-fighting, and vicious gossip. The classes definitely brought my attention to very real issues, and my later volunteer work with girls reiterated the difficulties they face – but why has this so often been our focus? Why do we focus on our dark side when there is so much wonderfulness to explore?

Perhaps this is the calling of women today – to bring to light the magnificence that is woman.

One thing I know is that I still have much to learn and experience about being female. But, I have begun to grow into my womanhood and feel more and more appreciative every day. I have discovered that when I allow myself to relax into my feminine, it is joyful and more fulfilling than anything else I may seek, perhaps because it is this comfortableness with my feminine nature that colors every other experience.

And, I have found that the more I appreciate my feminine nature, the more I appreciate men and the masculine nature. I value that there are marked differences between males and females and also that each of us has our own feminine traits and our own masculine traits. Like most endeavors in life, it is about finding our best balance. Perhaps when we embrace our feminine nature – and celebrate it – we will wholly express and fully step into our being. And, perhaps, as women do this collectively, it will lead to a balance of the masculine and feminine of the world.

It is here, with these inherent feminine qualities, that we begin this book. We have chosen to explore collaboration, creativity, intuition, nurturing, strength, trailblazing, and wisdom. We explore these topics through the voices of many women who inherently are saving the world – simply by being themselves. They are each representative of millions of women who do their part, every day, to make the world a better place, and it is my hope that millions more will read their stories and discover or remember their own beauty in being feminine.

It certainly is a wonderful time to be a woman!

– Caroline A. Shearer

collaboration

Juliette Gordon Low

"Ours is a circle of friends united by ideals." — Juliette Gordon Low

Juliette Gordon Low united thousands of people, young and old, to create one of the world's foremost youth development organizations, which has inspired girls to make the most of everything life has to offer for nearly 100 years.

....

Juliette Gordon Low was born Juliette "Daisy" Magill Kinzie Gordon on October 31, 1860, in Savannah, Georgia. Chronic ear infections during childhood caused her to lose much of her hearing in one ear. Then, at her 1886 wedding to William Mackay Low, a grain of traditional wedding rice lodged in her other ear, where it became infected and caused a complete loss of hearing on that side. Juliette and William were unhappily married for 19 years and lived in Low's native England. In 1905, Low died and left most of his estate to his mistress. Juliette spent the next few years traversing the globe.

In 1911, Juliette met Lord Robert Baden-Powell, the founder of the British Boy Scouts, which sparked her interest in youth scouting. Shortly after, Juliette founded the first Girl Scout troop, called Girl Guides, for underprivileged girls in Scotland and London. On March 12, 1912, she established the first American Girl Guides troop in Savannah. "I've got something for the girls of Savannah, and all of America, and all the world, and we're going to start it tonight!" she told a cousin over the phone. Eighteen girls comprised the first troop, with Margaret "Daisy Doots" Gordon, Juliette's niece and namesake, as first registered member. A mere one year later, the Girl Scouts of America was officially established. In 1915, it was incorporated with a national headquarters in Washington, D.C. In 1920, she was bestowed the deserved title of founder.

The American Girl Scouts welcomed girls of all backgrounds to learn about the wild outdoors, to develop independence and self-sufficiency, to learn traditional homemaking skills, and to prepare for the future. As new careers were becoming available to women, Girl Scout programs also taught about the arts, sciences, and business.

Juliette worked with devotion to secure support for the organization, build rapport with the community, grow the membership, and collaborate with similar youth service providers. She was known for her charm and eccentricity, her artistic and athletic talents, and her ability to perform headstands, which she demonstrated frequently – even once at a Girl Scout board meeting to display the new Girl Scout shoes.

Juliette was diagnosed with cancer in 1923, but she kept her illness a secret so as not to interfere with her work. When she succumbed to her illness, in 1927 at 66 years old, the Girl Scout membership totaled more than 168,000. Today, Girl Scouts has over 3.7 million current members, and more than 50 million former members. Though plagued by physical troubles throughout her life, Juliette persevered to found one of the largest and oldest youth development organizations in the world. On October 14, 2005, her life's work was immortalized as part of the Extra Mile Points of Light Volunteer Pathway in Washington, D.C.

....

• Founded Girl Scouts in 1912

• Founded Girl Scouts of America in 1913

• Organized the World Girl Scout Camp in New York in 1926

• Organized a convalescent hospital for wounded soldiers during the Spanish-American War

• Laid foundation for the World Association of Girl Guides and Girl Scouts

• Inducted into the National Women's Hall of Fame in Seneca Falls, New York, on October 28, 1979

Mary Harriman Rumsey

"It seems almost inhuman that we should live so close to suffering and poverty, that we should know of the deplorable conditions, and of the relief work that exists within a few blocks of our own home, and bear no part in this great life." – Mary Harriman Rumsey, in a 1906 Junior League annual report

Mary Harriman Rumsey defied society's expectations and showed the world the power of collaboration through the establishment of the Junior League for the Promotion of Settlement Movements (now the Junior League of New York City.)

....

Mary Harriman Rumsey was born in 1881, the eldest of six children born to railroad tycoon Edward Henry Harriman. Mary's family was exceptionally wealthy, and society expected her to enter society as a debutante on her 18th birthday. Instead, Mary studied Biology and Sociology at Barnard College. While she was there, she volunteered with immigrants at the College Settlement on Rivington Street in the slums of New York City's Lower East Side.

It was through her work at the College Settlement that Mary realized the power of collaboration. At age 19, Mary founded the Junior League for the Promotion of the Settlement Movements. The League's purpose was to encourage young, upper-class women to band together to help the poor and the underprivileged. Mary initially recruited 80 women, including Eleanor Roosevelt, to volunteer with the Junior League. Today, the Association of Junior Leagues International, Inc. consists of 292 Junior Leagues in four countries.

In addition to her work with the Junior League, Mary spent the 1920s and early 1930s distributing food and clothes to neighbors, formulating practical solutions for Depression-era problems, and engaging in politics and consumer advocacy. Unfortunately, Mary's revolutionary work ended early. She died in 1934, at the age of 53, from injuries sustained during a horseback riding accident.

....

- Social justice pioneer
- One of the first women of privilege to advocate for the poor
- Established the Junior League for the Promotion of Settlement Movements in 1901
- Co-founded the Welfare Council in the early 1920s
- Co-founder of Today magazine (now Newsweek)
- Chair of the Consumer Advisory Board of the National Recovery Administration, the United States' first consumer rights panel, 1933
- Co-authored the 1935 Social Security Act

Essays By Women

Collaborating to Create Change the Feminine Way

By Catrice M. Jackson, international empowerment speaker, global soul liberator, and bestselling author

....

It wasn't until my late thirties that I discovered the concept of the feminine and stopped thinking, feeling, and showing up in the world in masculine ways. You see, for most of my life, I thought being feminine meant being soft, weak, docile, dependent, and submissive. I had no idea that true femininity held a power and a strength all its own.

As a child, the absence of positive male role models in my life convinced me I had no time to be soft. Like my mother, grandmother, and aunts, I had to be strong and take care of myself. Not yet understanding true feminine strength, I thought this meant I had to be tough and go it alone. In short, I thought I had to act like a man.

As a result, I consciously chose to be independent and take charge of my life. While I physically looked feminine and took great interest in looking my best, I didn't feel feminine on the inside. Before I knew it, I had morphed into a tough, outspoken female who didn't take any crap from anyone! At the time, I was proud of who I was becoming because I thought I was standing in my power. I didn't recognize then how much I had to learn about what that meant.

Alienated from my own feminine nature, I became alienated from other females as well. During my junior high and high school years, I watched other girls as they used their outward appearances to seek, attract, and get boys; as they developed cliques and groups that ostracized others; and as they gossiped about and backstabbed each other. Competition seemed to be the name of the game, and I didn't want to participate in it. I didn't fully understand what was happening among us as girls then, but I knew – at a soul level – that it didn't feel right for me.

Though I wasn't overly competitive, I didn't understand the meaning of feminine collaboration. I didn't feel like I had anything in common with other girls. I had drawn the conclusion that girls (women) were catty, messy, and hateful. In fact, I intentionally kept my circle of female friends small and enjoyed hanging out with male friends more often.

But, something felt wrong. Somewhere deep inside of me I longed for deeper, soulful connections with women. I realize now that as teenage girls we all were either clueless about the power of being in our feminine or were driven by the power of being masculine. I realize we had no idea the pain, drama, and confusion we were creating in the lives of each other and in ourselves.

At 32 years old, I moved to a new city and started a women's support group out of my home. Though I was a mental health counselor, I had not experienced deep emotional, feminine connections with women outside of my work. Opening my home and my heart to these women felt like a big risk for me, but I was convinced I had something to teach them.

To my surprise, I became the student! I learned they were no different than me. I saw them in me and me in them. As I looked into their souls, I saw my own soul with new, loving eyes.

These women, whom I had imagined would gain so much from me, ended up teaching me how to share without shame and to be vulnerable enough to speak the truth even if I was afraid. Most importantly, they taught me that when women unite and create a sacred community of support, we can heal ourselves, our families, and the world, one woman at a time. Something within my soul was awakened. From somewhere deep inside, I heard a small voice softly say, "Welcome home, again."

It wasn't the first time I had heard that voice – the voice of my soul reminding me I am a daughter of the feminine. I had heard it before, but it had been a long time since I had experienced the feeling. Suddenly, it felt good to remember the truth.

In 1996, I had the opportunity to work as an AmeriCorps volunteer at a local domestic violence and sexual assault shelter. For three years, I advocated for, educated, counseled, and supported women survivors of abuse. Within months of taking the position, my soul was inspired and awakened to the movement of women's empowerment; it was something I had never experienced before. I loved every minute of my work, and I immediately knew it was what I was created to do on a soul level: to liberate, inspire, and empower the lives of women.

Unfortunately, although the job felt heaven-sent, the environment often reminded me of my teenage years. Though I worked with some amazing and passionate women who deeply cared about transforming the lives of women, ironically the environment was filled with competition, ego, and selfishness. We could not get ourselves out of the way to soulfully create the change we so desired to create. It was confusing – but I hoped there was a better way. On some unexplainable level deep within, I knew that, with simple faith, a power greater than us could facilitate the change we desired.

Sometime after, I began work at yet another women's empowerment program. For two years, I worked for a national women's program in my local community. Again, I loved it. Again, I heard my inner voice tell me I was home. Still, though I thoroughly enjoyed the work, the competitive and sometimes destructive actions of the other women – who were supposed to be working together for the greater good – were too much for me.

In early December 2007, my soul's calling finally hit me – like a ton of bricks! During a routine doctor's visit, I discovered my hemoglobin count was 5.5, with the normal range for women being 12-16. My vital organs were not getting enough oxygen, and I was, in the words of my doctor, "walking dead."

My soul battled between the words of my late grandmother, who had taught me it was a sin to take body parts from another human being, and my spirit, which knew I had a purpose to fulfill and a destiny to live. I experienced what I call a Soul Eruption, a deep and profound moment when you know for sure who you are and why you are here.

Afraid, I prayed and chose to take the blood, vowing to God that I would live and fully carry out His calling for my life. I made a soul commitment to live the rest of my life pioneering a global movement that would liberate, inspire, and empower women.

I left the hospital on a Friday, contemplated my life all day Saturday, and on Sunday sat down and wrote a resignation letter that would be the beginning of my life's work as it is today. On Monday, I submitted the letter with no fear or regret. In fact, it was one of the most soul-liberating experiences of my life. I left the organization to pursue my soul dream of becoming an entrepreneur, who speaks and coaches to inspire women on my own terms. I knew then that all of my life lessons and experiences with women – good, bad, and indifferent – happened for a reason. They were preparation for my plan and purpose to teach and inspire women to come together without shame or fear, to create a soul community where women could embrace their feminine selves to connect and collaborate, to heal the lives of women around the world. I didn't know exactly how or when this would occur, but I trusted in the why and used what God gave me to lead women into their feminine greatness.

It has been five years since then. Five years in which I have been seeking to deeply understand and embrace the beauty of the feminine. I've come to know that it is our most powerful space to be in as women. We were created to love, nurture, create, commune, co-create, and collaborate within communities to care for, inspire, and heal humanity. While we must seek harmony among our feminine and masculine energies, when we live from, operate within, and engage with others from our feminine source, we are being all that we were created to be.

Competition amongst women takes us out of the natural flow of life. When we compete with one another, there is strife, struggle, and resistance; we are driven by our egos to conquer instead of connecting and collaborating. There are times when we must be driven, focused, strong, and in charge, but not to the extent that we hurt others and lack compassion for the human spirit.

Universally, there is no reason to compete. You are enough, I am enough, and there is enough for all of us. Once I soulfully digested this truth, I gracefully could stand in the power of my feminine and honor the feminine within other women. Amazing things happen when we do this.

My life's journey has taught me the significant difference between being a woman and living in the feminine. In my opinion, living as a woman is a physical manifestation; living from our feminine is a soul experience anchored in who we innately are. Living in the feminine and collaborating from this space allows us to care for ourselves, care for others, and impact the world with the collective power of connectedness and compassion. Choosing feminine collaboration in our lives, work, and mission decreases competition, lessens the struggle, and affords us more ease and grace. As we travel our journey, I share with you a perspective to consider as you consciously embrace your feminine self:

When a woman steps into her feminine, she realizes that her soul is the most beautiful part of who she is. When a woman deeply discovers her feminine, she honors the essence of who she is from the inside out. When a woman embraces her feminine, she soulfully knows she is embracing the feminine souls of women around the world. When a woman owns her feminine, she embodies her innate ability to care for, love, and nurture all who enter her space, especially herself. When a woman honors her feminine, she is not afraid to be comforting, compassionate, sensual, and soft for fear of being seen as weak. When a woman engages in her feminine, she honors the feminine in other women and creates communities where the feminine is celebrated and not just tolerated. When a woman leads from her feminine, she blazes the trail of her destiny by shining the light of her soul, thus creating a path for other women to follow.

We are the pulse of the world, and when we live from our feminine, we pulsate powerful vibrations that echo beyond what we can imagine. The feminine spirit of collaboration is at the core of who we are; to engage in contrast weakens our collective vibration. When we come together as women with the pure intention to collaborate, to create greater good, we not only heal and empower ourselves, we enhance and transform the human experience.

I hope you choose to let go of insecurity, shame, fear, and judgment. I hope you choose to see and honor the feminine in other women. I hope you choose to go forth knowing with every cell of your body that you are enough, she is enough, we are enough, just the way we are. I challenge you to trust in your value and your gifts with full confidence and to know that there is no competition because there is enough for all of us.

. . . .

Catrice M. Jackson, international empowerment speaker, P-Spot passionista, international bestselling author, and global leader of the GetNAKED Movement, fearlessly liberates the souls of women worldwide. Catrice serves up delicious life recipes that inspire women to *Get NAKED*, discover their juicy spot, own it, celebrate it, and sprinkle it into the world. Catriceology, Catrice's signature life empowerment brand, is a unique concoction infused with a savvy and sassy flavor that helps women experience the freedom to be fearless, fierce, and fired up in their lives. Catrice's global mission is to create, cultivate, and sustain a worldwide community of brave, bold, and brilliant women who live in their P-Spot by abandoning what they "should" be and becoming who they are. Catrice is passionate about helping women feel the pulse of purpose, experience profound peace, and press PLAY on their passions for more pleasure and prosperity.

Catrice's Mantra: "Doing it my way, with no regrets or the need to ask permission, gracefully being soul-led, covered in favor, serving up the Catriceology flavor and doing it fearlessly, free, and simply just being me." Experience Catriceology at www.catriceology.com.

Competing to Win, Collaborating to Live

By Kiva Leatherman, founder and president of the Wise Women Network and host of Contact Talk Radio's "A Woman's Worth"

....

I never really learned how to share. An only child of a take-no-prisoners mother, I learned to fend for myself, by myself, from an early age. Power and competition were the things for which I'd been raised.

By the time she was 26, my mother was a newspaper editor in Tucson, Arizona. When I was five, she left my father, packed us up for New York City, hired a nanny, and went to work on the night shift copy-desk for one of the largest newspapers in the country. She was fierce and ambitious. In no time, she was the fashion editor and flew to Paris and Milan for fashion shows.

She was, and is, an awesome mother. Not in the June Cleaver sense of awesome, more like a Martha Stewart type of awesome … without the cookies. I believe she is one of the true founders of the belief that women "can and should have it all." She never missed a basketball game, she cooked dinner five or six nights a week, and she taught me that I could and should be anything I wanted to be. She is extraordinary, and it was extraordinarily difficult to live up to her expectations. But, I knew from a very early age that I would do whatever I could to try.

When I was six or seven, my mother asked me if I'd rather go to Hebrew school or ballet class. There was no doubt what the "right" answer was; my mother's intonation made it very clear which one she thought I should choose, and so I am the most un-Jewish Jewish woman I know. Ballet became my religion.

I wasn't the best, and it was clear by the age of 12 that my Eastern European hips weren't going to cooperate, but I was determined. I slept with my legs like a frog to improve my turnout and viciously scoped out my competition at annual auditions for "The Nutcracker." But, my hips would not cooperate, and eventually I quit. If I couldn't be the best – well, then I didn't want anything to do with it.

I started going to a school that specialized in theatre dance. I was in New York, after all, and if I couldn't be the best ballerina, then maybe, just maybe, I could be on Broadway by the time I was 16. See, my mom didn't raise me to be in a dance recital – she raised me to be a star!

I was as fierce and competitive and obsessive as ever, but I still wasn't the best. So I quit.

I went to college in the Midwest. There, even though I hadn't danced in over a year, I decided to go to the auditions for the dance department. I viciously scoped out my competition, as always, scoffed at their non-New York trained techniques, and fought my way into the production as the only freshman. There, I was the best.

The piece I was cast in was a collaboration, six women and a choreographer working together to create something amazing. I fell in love with all of them. I began to see strengths in them that I knew I didn't have. I was amazed at the ingenuity of our group. I remember playing around with my friend Amy, who was lying on the floor, spent. I did a handstand over her shoulders. She lifted her legs in jest, and I rolled my body down her legs as she lowered them. "Whoa, let's do that again." We did. Eventually all of us did, one couple after the other, across the stage. It was honestly the most powerful and ambitious piece I'd ever danced in. It was my first taste of the possibility of authentic collaboration – it was bliss.

But, a funny thing happened to my competitive spirit once I knew I was the best. I stopped going to my dance classes, made lame excuses, and looked down at everyone else's diligence and perseverance. And, soon enough, I was no longer the best. So I quit.

Off I went into the big, bad world of high finance, and boy was I fierce! I was one of three women on a sales desk of fifty. It was me against them – and by "them," I mean the two other women. I called my mom for advice on how to eat their lunch. She shared strategies on how to outmaneuver my peers, ingratiate myself with my bosses, and navigate power struggles.

The apple doesn't fall far from the tree, and by the time I was 26, I was an account executive with a six-figure salary. I loved the game, and I was good at it. But, I was not to be messed with. I had earned a reputation of being able to hold my own with the big boys. And, I'll admit that I knew exactly what I was doing when I played the part of the sweet, young blonde. Kill them with kindness – the faker the better. Blech. It hurts my heart to even write that. But, the truth is that in the world of investment management, the strategies worked. I gained the respect of my male peers. On the outside, those strategies made me a success.

I call those my Easter egg years. I was all glittery and decorated on the outside, but inside I was empty. I was brittle. I was so alone.

The world of an outside sales woman is a rough and lonely existence. My perception was that other women hated me. After all, in the finance industry most of the other women were assistants, and I was on top. And, if I was too friendly with the men ... well, we all know about the perception that creates. Good thing I'd learned to fend for myself.

But, I hadn't – not really.

I would sit in my big closet filled with Ellie Tahari suits, Louis Vuitton bags, and Prada shoes and cry. I would go to bars and pretend I was waiting to meet someone – and drink by myself. I would even fake the phone call of my "late" friend, letting me know she wouldn't be making it after all.

But, I'd won the game. I was the best. I could eat your lunch. All. By. Myself.

I've written often about the outcome of my Easter egg years. I cracked. Actually, I quit. But, it was worse, I didn't actually quit – who quits that kind of money? I just stopped doing the work. And, I got fired.

And, finally, I stopped playing the game. I stopped trying to get the part, or eat anyone's lunch, or run with the big boys. For a year, I just was. I did my best to parent my young children and convince my husband (poor guy ... thought he'd married a winner!) that the stay-at-home mom thing was my life's calling. I tried to convince myself I hadn't ruined everything, even if I felt washed up at 35.

Lucky for me, my mom didn't raise me to be June Cleaver. She raised me to be Martha Stewart. She raised me to be resilient and resourceful. She raised me to pick myself up. She raised me to be a star.

So, eventually, the idea that had been bouncing around in my head for years – to teach women about their money in a way that was compassionate and empathetic – formed into reality and became the Wise Women Network.

From the beginning, I knew that the last thing I wanted was to do it alone. It was going to be collaborative. I remembered those years of creating something extraordinary when I danced with amazing women in college. I remembered how light I felt when I let go of my ego and honored my fellow dancers' brilliance. I knew I was going to have to learn how to share. As in share the work, share the reward, share the glory.

Easy to say, but in practice I had no idea what sharing felt like; I just knew I wanted to do it. I wish I could tell you the lessons were easy, and that, in a moment, I learned to collaborate with feminine grace. But, they weren't, and I didn't.

My first attempt at collaboration came in the form of bringing in a partner to help create my vision. This is hard to admit, but I thought I could do all the dreaming, and she could do all the working. That plan didn't work out so well. She ended up being embroiled in a messy divorce, and I ended up doing the visioning, lifting, creating, building ... everything. It was the best thing that could have happened to me in terms of changing internal beliefs I had about my work ethic. But, I hadn't found bliss again, yet.

Thankfully, life has a way of leading us right where we need to go. I walked into my first mastermind group (a collective of people with like-minded goals formed with the intention of supporting and inspiring each other,) and there was another woman with a financial background. Cue: hackles up. I was ready to go to the mat with that woman, who is now not only a dear friend but someone I admire and look up to, just to prove I was the best.

What a shock it was when I realized she had no interest in competing with me! She authentically wanted to help me succeed. And, then, I met another woman like her, and another, and my jaded worldview softened. I softened. I started wearing prettier clothes, and I stopped straightening my naturally wavy hair. I felt safe. I felt loved. I felt soft-boiled.

Here's the best part: I don't have to be the best at anything anymore. I don't even have to try. I don't even want to be the best. I just want to be me.

By embracing collaboration, I was able to regain my financial success without sacrificing my soul. It is beyond fun, as in pinch-myself-I-cannot-believe-this-is-my-life fun, to get to work with the women that I get to work with. We are creating projects and programs together that change the course of women's and children's lives. We are far more extraordinary together than we could ever be alone.

Before I had a clue of what Wise Women Network would become, I wrote a poem about the vision I had for what we could be together:

Our ideal is empowerment. Collaboration. Inspiration. Support.
There is no judgment here. There is no competition here.
As women – we have the resources and the desire to enrich our own lives and the lives of those around us.
We are strong.
We are industrious.
We are Wise.

I am laughing right now because I didn't even know the depths of what I wrote when I wrote it. I had yet to discover what I even meant. But, clearly, my soul knew exactly what I needed.

···

Kiva Leatherman is the founder and president of the Wise Women Network, which inspires and teaches women to live up to their worth – emotionally, physically, and financially. She is also the host of Contact Talk Radio's "A Woman's Worth." As a speaker, Kiva encourages women to know themselves, to know about their money, and to stop living vicariously through others – to achieve success and happiness on their terms. Kiva was formerly a sales vice president with a major investment firm, where she managed a territory that generated over $100 million in annual sales. Although the investment business was definitely a boys' club, Kiva found a way to succeed with grace, humor, and feminine strength. Her presentations on women and investing laid the groundwork for what eventually became Wise Workshops and her personal mission to ensure that women are in charge of their own money, their own time, and the decisions they make regarding their nutrition and health. She teaches women to create a framework for success, which gives them the power and freedom to live well.

Kiva graduated with degrees in Psychology and Performing Arts from Washington University in St. Louis. She loves teaching women to get their groove on through dance and is a certified fitness trainer. www.wiseworkshops.com

Setting the Stage for Collaboration

By Dea Shandera, "Zen Executive," film producer, and media consultant

···

Nothing in the universe can act alone. The instruments of a symphony; the cells, microbes, and nutrients of a human body; the planets, stars, and physical forces of a galaxy – everything we know works collaboratively and in harmony with everything else. When harmony is absent, destruction occurs. By working in harmony with the universe, we tap into the divine nature of the world and give our own lives momentum and depth.

Collaboration is, in essence, a birthing process. Our own feminine spirit, the part of ourselves that is the creator of life, understands it takes a village to do anything of great importance. Collaboration has the power to push us toward places and accomplishments that are nearly impossible to reach from a false sense of isolation. Collaboration between people was very likely born out of this realization.

As women, collaboration is often part of our intrinsic nature. With a nurturing spirit, we can grow this nature within ourselves and become positive role models for others. Collaboration is the spirit within us all that leads us to co-create, to birth something new. It is the driving force behind evolution, creation, sustenance, and movement. Everyone – men and women alike – possess both feminine and masculine qualities, and we all can find joy and bring about peace by working together.

Building a successful collaboration requires both internal and external harmony. The desire to collaborate and the ability to take part in something that shares talents and creativity, without the need to control or cause discord, without the need for singular fame and recognition, without the ego, enables all things to be possible. Just as harmony in music cannot be achieved if there is a sour note, harmony in a person or a group cannot be reached if there is anger, frustration, or if the channels of communication are closed.

True collaboration, a product of harmony, is thus at the core of peace – both our own inner peace and world peace. To work together, we must be open to and build a place where ideas can be exchanged – and discussed – freely, where criticism and critique can be given and accepted gracefully, and where progress can be made. This requires us to approach one another with respect and goodwill.

Sometimes, a member of a group will not begin a project with respect for his or her peers, but it is still vital for others to maintain respect for that person and recognize his or her negativity for what it is – perhaps just an early step on that person's spiritual journey. Humans are spiritual beings having a temporary, earthly experience. Harmony in any collaboration is thus dependent on recognizing everyone as a spiritual pilgrim, many of whom may not yet recognize their own divinity. Forgiving ourselves and others when we make mistakes or do not act in a harmonious manner is a key component of creating an environment where collaboration can thrive. Finding a partner who can teach us to be more forgiving and easier going, and who draws out the best in us, is the true heart of collaboration.

Brent, my life partner, has been the one to teach me about the ultimate magic in the collaborative spirit, that teamwork can be miraculous, and that every-thing is perfect. Collaborations with this same fire do not have to be with a lover or a husband, though. They can be found in any kindred spirit – friends, family, co-workers, children, even people we've just met. We must allow our intuition to guide us.

Collaborations often start from scratch, and it can sometimes be intimidating to find a harmonious space in new territory. When Brent and I partnered for the first time, it was a beautiful, spontaneous combustion. He was working as a contract employee for major corporations, and when we were paired in business, we began to see the unlimited synergies in what we do and in the gifts we came into life to share.

We started working together. I handled the traditional marketing and public relations aspect of our work; he took care of the technical and social media part. We easily saw how the merging of our ideas led to our ability to recognize the greatness and the potential in each other. Our relationship as a couple came first, but it was the addition of us as co-creators in business that gave us unlimited opportunities to experience collaboration at the core of both aspects of our beautiful relationship.

Sometimes, we work with clients where the energies are not in alignment so it's difficult to find harmony in the project, and completing the work feels a bit like pulling teeth. We recently finished two projects where the essence of the energy between the clients and us was not one of collaboration. Because we come from a place where collaboration is at the core of everything we do, it can be extra challenging when we meet people who don't operate this way. If this happens, we have to work harder to find a level playing field where harmonious collaboration can begin to occur. But, once we find it, success happens every time. When people don't find that ground where they can communicate and work together, success will be rare.

The key to collaborating with anyone is to understand that working collaboratively is a choice. The choice must be proactive, and it must be committed to for the duration of a project or undertaking. Problems will arise, but there is always a way for everyone's needs to be met. Sometimes, figuring out how to accomplish that can be the first act in the creation of a successful collaboration.

If you have people coming together who are trying to accomplish something, for example, at a church, the project doesn't have to just feel like work. Enter into the endeavor with a positive outlook and a goal of enjoyment. Different members of the group may have different ideas about what constitutes a workload or how to get started, but if you are committed to being a team and having a successful outcome, then that intention, if everyone chooses it, can create real and meaningful collaboration.

It's best when the overarching goal of any collaboration is to create a sense of oneness between you and your partner(s), to close separations, and to bridge any gaps that divide you from each other and your goal. Many women are uniquely gifted at this because we are often innately intuitive and empathetic – two blessings that enable us to quickly pick up on what a person is feeling and respond appropriately.

Working with new people can seem daunting, but a diversity of viewpoints, perspectives, thoughts, feelings, personalities, and skills will bring fresh thoughts and novel approaches to any task. It may seem stressful if a partner has a vocal and differing opinion than your own, but set ego aside and listen fully before interjecting or disagreeing. Universal or unconditional love is an important component of successful collaboration. When our hearts and our ears are open and we are ready to co-create, only then is the stage set for collaboration on every level.

There are difficult people to work with in the world, but, at heart, everyone is filled with goodness. If someone is causing difficulties when trying to work together, consider that he or she might be in some sort of pain. Invite this person to hear the intentions of the group so that the common good can be brought into focus, and a sense of harmony can be restored – or initiated – within the environment.

If that doesn't work, then one person who is gifted with compassion and a nurturing spirit should approach the person and have a talk, acknowledge the person's wonderful strengths, and let the person know he or she can jump in whenever it feels right. Remind this person that everyone will win if the group is successful, and that it isn't about any one individual; it's about the group and the group's goals so grudges and annoyances must be left outside. There will be times when that is not enough – when someone just doesn't want to be a part of the collaborative process. When that happens, the only thing to do is to gently and lovingly take that person out of the process. But, only after you've tried everything to include them.

Because my beloved and I live and work together, we collaborate personally and professionally 24/7. This presents unlimited opportunities for co-creation that have fulfilled us beyond our wildest dreams. We work together – understanding each other's needs, motives, background, and desired goals in all things – to figure out a path that enables us to problem solve and create together. In this regard, harmony through collaboration is created in our personal and professional lives, and, as a result, within ourselves. The world will be an inherently better place when we all learn to co-create like this because with full collaboration comes ultimate success. And, with that success comes collaboration's truest reward – a sense of peace and harmony for everyone involved.

Peace is created when two (or more) forces learn to work and exist together, whether those forces are different people or even conflicting aspects of our own personalities. When we master this peace and collaboration, a sense of harmony and accomplishment is gained. In this way, harmony comes out of collaboration, and collaboration creates harmony, both inside and out. Here's to a future where compassion and collaboration are ever-present!

. . . .

Dea Shandera realized long ago that she is a spiritual being having a human experience. Dubbed by many as the "Zen Executive," she is a highly re-garded and seasoned creative entertainment industry leader, having served tenures over 25 years at Paramount Pictures, The Walt Disney Company, and MGM. Her most recent post was as executive vice president of worldwide marketing for MGM Television. Dea has consulted in every area of the entertainment/media business – from publicity and marketing for books, movies, and television to film and video production and film distribution, as well as book publishing. She always has been a champion of stories and projects that celebrate the human spirit and inspire people to be their greatest. Some of her consulting clients include Michael Bernard Beckwith, Agape Media International, Waterside Productions, Trifecta Entertainment and Media, The Rainbow Bridge, Spirit Rising Productions, Annapurna Studios, Rocky Mountain Pictures, Sony Pictures Home Entertainment, Gener8Xion Entertainment, and authors James Redfield, William Gladstone, Dannion Brinkley, Ervin Laszlo, Judith Diana Winston, Susan Hall, Jesse Dylan, Sharmen Lane, Kristen Moeller, Annie Burnside, and Peter Anthony. Dea lives and works in Southern California with her beloved life and business partner, visionary author, entrepreneur, and social media genius Brent Hunter.

I am Collaborative.

1. I am authentic in my interactions with others.

2. I discover ways of interacting in which everyone benefits.

3. I recognize that the process of collaboration opens doors to synergy, synchronicity, and expansion.

4. I release my need to win or be better than others and, instead, wish for success for all.

5. I appreciate that differences, while they may appear challenging, are opportunities for an idea – and everyone working on it – to grow.

creativity

Louisa May Alcott

"Far away there in the sunshine are my highest aspirations. I may not reach them, but I can look up and see their beauty, believe in them, and try to follow where they lead." – Louisa May Alcott

Louisa May Alcott dipped from a deep well of creativity, which was fed by a childhood in the wild New England countryside in the shadow of literary giants and realized through determination and dedication to her craft.

....

Louisa May Alcott, born on November 29, 1832, in Germantown, Pennsylvania, was one of four sisters born to a poor but educationally ambitious family. Her father, Bronson Alcott, was well-known as an innovative educator and a member of an elite transcendental philosophical group that included Henry David Thoreau and Ralph Waldo Emerson.

Most of Louisa's childhood was spent in Concord and Boston, Massachusetts, but the family moved often to accommodate Bronson's academic, philosophic, and career endeavors. Louisa was a tomboy considered wild by her parents, who once sent her away because she was too difficult to manage. Later, Louisa reflected on her departure from traditional female values, "No boy could be my friend 'til I had beaten him in a race," she claimed, "and no girl if she refused to climb trees, leap fences."

She was passionate about writing from childhood, with a vast imagination often expressed through melodramas enacted by herself, friends, and sisters. Playing a shrinking violet or damsel in distress was not to Louisa's liking – she preferred the "lurid" roles in her productions, "the villains, ghosts, bandits, and disdainful queens."

Despite the joy found with her family, it was undeniable that Louisa was growing up in poverty; her father was plagued by debts and failed business ventures. Louisa knew she would have to contribute to the family's income, and proclaimed at 15, "I'll be rich and famous and happy before I die, see if I won't!" The time period was not known for embracing ambitious young women, but Louisa did not intend to let that detour her. "I will make a battering-ram of my head and make my way through this rough and tumble world," she said.

And, make her way she did. Her first attempts at serious writing were met with adversity, but Louisa continued to develop her craft, undeterred, and began publishing her stories under the pseudonym "A. M. Barnard." When the Civil War erupted, Alcott became an active abolitionist and volunteered briefly as a nurse at the Union Hotel Hospital in Washington, D.C. Her experiences as a nurse were published as the popular "Hospital Sketches," but also left her in poor health for the remainder of her life.

With the 1868 publication of "Little Women," Louisa catapulted into fame. Her iconic character, Jo March, was modeled after her own wild days as a child on farms in New England and became one of the first strong, independent female heroines for juveniles in the history of American literature. Before her death, Louisa authored over 30 books and collections of short stories. On March 1, 1888, Louisa visited her father following his stroke. "I am going up," he said. "Come with me." "Oh, I wish I could," she replied. He died on March 4, and she followed shortly after on March 6. She is buried in Sleepy Hollow cemetery in Concord beneath a grave bearing a Civil War veteran's marker.

....

- Pioneered women's rights through self-sufficiency and political activism
- Part of the New England school of Transcendental thinkers and philosophers through her father, Bronson Alcott
- Remained completely independent in an era when women were expected to marry and be coddled

Edna St. Vincent Millay

"Soar, eat ether, see what has never been seen; depart, be lost, but climb." – Edna St. Vincent Millay

Edna St. Vincent Millay married feminine vitality and liberty with beauty and sensitivity through her poetry. She explored themes and terrain both in verse and life that opened new pathways for future generations of women.

....

Edna St. Vincent Millay was born February 22, 1892, in Rockland, Maine, into a troubled home with two sisters. She was raised by a single mother after her father was asked to leave the family home in 1899. The absence of a father did not handicap Millay's early talent, though, as her mother entrenched her daughters in music and literature, while encouraging them to be strong and independent.

Her first major poem, "Renascence," was published in 1912; it brought her instant acclaim and a scholarship to Vassar College. The poem, with themes focused on spiritual interment and rebirth through the cycling seasons, combines naiveté and profundity with both modern and archaic diction.

At Vassar, Millay became involved with the theatre, which inspired several of her verse plays. Millay gained notoriety as a heartbreaker, including for her relationships with women, whose influence can be seen in her poems that celebrate feminine beauty.

Following her graduation from Vassar, Millay moved to Greenwich Village in New York and published her first book, "Renascence and Other Poems" in 1917. Her life in New York, occupying a small attic space and writing for any publisher or editor she could find, was the epitome of Bohemian. Of herself and her fellow writers and friends, Millay said they were all "very, very poor and very, very merry."

Millay continued her involvement in theatre with the Provincetown Players and befriended or romanced many of the influential writers and actors of the day, refusing marriage proposals and continuing to write the poetry that would win her further acclaim.

In 1920, she published "A Few Figs from Thistles," a book of verse that gained notoriety for its descriptions of female sexuality and feminism. Her most recognizable quatrain, titled "First Fig," comes from this collection:

My candle burns at both ends;
It will not last the night;
But ah, my foes, and oh, my friends--
It gives a lovely light!

She won the Pulitzer Prize in 1923 for her fourth book, "The Harp Weaver." That same year, Millay accepted a marriage proposal from Eugen Boissevain, a progressive feminist who strongly supported Millay's career. They remained married for 26 years, until Boissevain's death in 1949. Millay died in 1950.

. . . .

• Wrote and acted in her own plays, including The Princess Marries the Page and Aria da Capo

• Won a $100 prize from Poetry: A Magazine of Verse for "The Bean-Stalk" in 1920

• First woman to win the Pulitzer Prize for poetry in 1923

• Wrote opera for the Metropolitan Opera of New York

• Politically active and believed staunchly in freedom and equal rights

• Elected to the National Institute of Arts and Letters in 1929

• Elected to the American Academy of Arts and Letters in 1940

 Essays By Women

Appreciating the Power of Creativity

By Terry Grahl, founder and visionary for Enchanted Makeovers and
award-winning interior decorator, activist, and author

....

Once Upon a Time

When I was a little girl, taking care of my handmade dolls, I felt like I was
taking care of myself. As I tucked my precious doll into bed each night, I had
to make sure her arms were comfortable and legs were covered so she could
stay warm. I knew in my heart she was happy because I nurtured her the
way I loved to be nurtured. I made sure every piece of her hair was in place,
brushed away from her delicate face. My doll needed to shine, just like me.

I wanted the world to see her beauty and light through her eyes and mine.
I loved my doll, and my doll loved me. I could feel the crafter had sewn her
story into the heart of the doll. Each handmade outfit and hand-embroidered
face embodied the creator. The precious eyes must have helped the crafter "look"
back on what truly made her happy. The hair reminded me that no matter
life's circumstances, they could be changed. Years later, I never thought that
dolls would be the one thing I would need to release from my life in order to
fulfill a much bigger plan, one I could never have imagined.

When the pitter-patter of my children's footsteps left my house for the hallways
of elementary and junior high school, I began to focus on finishing the last
details of our home. This included hand painting a cobblestone driveway
to remind myself that life is a journey and that we should always put footsteps to our prayers. I painted my front door purple and covered my purple arch
in my driveway with red roses to remind me to never forget we can be shining
stars. Wooden handmade shutters embraced the windows on my home and
became the eyes to my future. The garden was filled with hand-painted
gnomes that spoke volumes to me every day. I heard, "Believe, believe my
child in everything your eyes can't see . . . never lose your child-like faith."
The very moment I painted the last, loving detail on my home, it was transformed
into "Hope," and I was ready to share my creativity and imagination with

the world.

As I stood staring at my collection of dolls, I knew I would have to sell them in order to start my own interior decorating business. A rush of emotions came over me, and I felt as though I was somehow giving myself away. I remember thinking, "Stop being so foolish, they are only dolls!" But, were they? They held the memories of nurturance and the power of my imagination. They also represented the compassion and nurturing I could ultimately share with others. I was scared and full of fear, yet so excited for the new journey ahead of me. The selling of my dolls would be the birth of a new chapter in my life.

The Business

In November 2005, I founded Terry's Enchanted Cottage, a decorating business that ultimately would be more about giving women hope than decorating. I was so excited when I received a call from my very first client, Jeannie.

As I visited her house, I remember feeling an enormous amount of pain and suffering. My instincts told me that something was not right. All of the walls were white, a blank slate that represented a lack of vision for the future. Flea market treasures were placed at odd locations with price tags still attached. As a flea market fanatic, I believe when you purchase someone else's treasures, you have to respect them, clean them, and then own them.

The dots began to connect and form much greater plans.

The transformation of Jeannie's home would prove to be more than paint, pretty accessories, vintage furniture, and curtains. It was actually an awakening of Jeannie's spirit. It was time to bring color into her life, which would become a bright light of hope. New black-and-white-checkered flooring represented a new path and new beginnings.

When we were done, I asked her three very important questions: "What does your home really represent to you? How do you envision your future? Do you believe you can create your own world?" I suggested she actually name her home. She called it "High Hopes." She now had a place to create her own future, believe in the impossible, and nurture herself.

The Dots are Connecting

In December 2006, one year after I opened my decorating business, Jeannie stood at her make-up station and listened to a client tell her about a house he drove past every day, a house that "stood out" to him. The client told Jeannie it was a sign on the home that stood out the most. It read, "High Hopes." Jeannie, suddenly overcome with emotion, shouted, "That is my home, that is my home!" She then told him about the home's transformation process and about how I helped her heal her home and ultimately herself. His response changed everything.

"Do you think she would paint a wall at the shelter?" he asked.

It turned out that the client, David, was the event coordinator for a women's shelter. His question led to what ultimately became a magical golden thread of hope that would touch many lives.

The Visit

I made a visit to the shelter in January 2007, but not without fear as my companion. I didn't know what to expect; I had never been to a shelter. As with all the consultations I conducted with private clients in my decorating business, I took photos to assist with planning and visualization. I wasn't sure if I would actually accept the volunteer job, and I was leaning toward "probably not" when I began to climb the staircase to the women's dorm.

As I climbed, my heart began to race. The chipped steps, dark stairway, and dirty windows reminded me of a path to nowhere. I opened the metal door to a dorm that slept 30 women and their children for one year. I immediately began to feel the enormous amount of negative energy that surrounded every broken piece, pieces which seemed to represent lost dreams and lost youth. Walls were held together by duct tape, which represented barriers in life. Stained mattresses, used prison bunk beds, and nursing home bedspreads were reminders of painful pasts, bad choices, and death.

"Why am I here?" I asked myself. "And how could I possibly change all of this?"

A Dream Remembered

A week passed, and I still felt a lingering despair from the knowledge of how the women and children lived. I began to reflect upon my own expectations for my life, the dreams of a child, and the wisdom my mother instilled in my siblings and me. My mother taught us that decorating didn't need to be motivated by money and that, by relying on our own creativity and vision, each home improvement act could be a selfless act of love. For my mother, making a home where her five children felt safe and where our spirits could soar was as important as keeping us fed and clothed. How could the women and children in the shelter realize their dreams in such conditions?

A Path to a New Beginning

As I presented a plan to the group of women and the shelter's staff, I was overcome with emotion. Transforming the shelter would require more than my creative skills; it would require me to pull on strengths I did not even know I had. I would have to find, organize, collaborate with, and lead enthusiastic crafters, sewers, mural artists, painters, and donors nationwide to help carry out my vision.

My creative juices immediately began to flow as I met for the first time with a mural artist at the shelter. I began to envision the stairway as an Enchanted Forest. A forest filled with hidden messages, mother birds feeding their babies, and other birds singing praise for the tender loving care the mothers were expressing. The women and children would now walk through a forest to get to their dorm.

The windows, wiped clean of the past, sparkled. They would become the eyes to the soul. Twig shutters were attached on each side of the windows, and custom flower boxes made by craftsmen were filled with geraniums. The top landing of the staircase would feel as though the women and children had just found a cottage tucked away in the woods, "A Hopeful Haven." The cold metal door would be painted to look like a welcoming vintage screen door. The walls were painted a warm buttery yellow, the color of their cottage. A painted mailbox next to their front door would allow only positive messages. Handmade chimes would cast away any negative energy. Even the doormat was more than just a place to wipe feet – it would be a reminder before entering "A Hopeful Haven" of the choice we all have to wipe away our mistakes and start new.

When we finished, the mural artist's eyes filled with tears. "I have never been given permission to nurture the child from within," he said.

"I'm giving you permission," I responded. "It is time to share yourself with others."

The Dorm Awaits: The Power of Handmade

I have always believed that "handmade" heals as it carries the love and positive energy of the creator. I was determined that the women and children of the shelter would no longer lie down with worn blankets – only quilts made with love by human hands. The quilts would become hope. I envisioned the pillowcases as safe places for each woman and child to lay her head. The crafters would embroider ASK*BELIEVE*RECEIVE on every pillowcase as a daily reminder that nothing is impossible.

Custom lamps with shades filled with vintage mother-of-pearl buttons would represent each woman and her courage on the new journey ahead. The light would help guide her way. Hand painted journals made by artists would be a powerful way for every woman to write down her thoughts and remind herself of the negative ones that used to control her life. The new paint covered the past tears, and opened the door (the heart) to a better future. Curtains – prayed over, cried over, and filled with love by the seamstress – were made for each window. Each curtain represented the seamstress's meditation "she is me," a meditation which aligned her thoughts with the golden thread ... a thread that connects us all.

Six months later, the makeover was complete. "I feel like I'm living in a dollhouse," said one of the women. The transformation was amazing. Even more amazing to me was that I had found my true calling. I wanted to use all of my talents, creativity, and skills to provide refuge, solace, inspiration, and hope to women and children living in shelters, as well as the volunteers.

A Leap of Faith

I felt God wanted to use me for His glory. We made a deal with each other on the day I made the decision to "paint that wall." I asked that He continue to provide for the needs of my family (food and a roof over our heads,) and His request was, "Glorify Me."

I believe that whenever we tap into our imagination, we nurture the child within. It's even more powerful when we take what we have created and give it away. We are sharing ourselves, baring our souls, and living a more authentic, feminine life.

....

Terry Grahl is the founder and visionary of Enchanted Makeovers, an award-winning non-profit organization committed to transforming shelters into places that inspire psychological and behavioral changes – places where women and children rebuilding their lives are reminded every day that we all hold the "golden ticket" to transforming our dreams into reality. She's also a wife, mother to four children, activist, author, award-winning interior decorator, and a woman on a mission to inspire people to dream and follow their hearts, to see each other truly as an extension of one's self.

Terry founded Enchanted Makeovers in 2007, and she has been on an extraordinary journey ever since. Her creativity, child-like innocence, and whimsy are reflected throughout the mission. Terry was named People Magazine and Major League Baseball's "All-Star Among Us" in 2010 out of 7,500 nominations nationwide. Within a week, she was standing on the Los Angeles baseball field watching celebrity Sheryl Crow present a video on her non-profit at the MLB All-Star game. National press includes People Magazine, First for Women, Woman's World, Better Homes and Gardens Quilts & More, Martha Stewart, Country Almanac, Paint Magic, Redbook, Cottages & Bungalows, Ladies Home Journal, PBS, and Oprah Winfrey Show. www.enchantedmakeovers.org

Creativity and the Feminine Energy

By Carmel Rivello Maguire, author of the upcoming book, "Motherhood, Marketing, and Marinara" and speaker on corporate communications, leadership, attitude, and validation

....

Webster's Dictionary defines the word "create" as the quality of being creative ... imagination, ingenuity, invention, to bring into existence, to invest in a new form, to produce, to beget.

Our creative, feminine energy, our spirit in flames, has brought me on a journey to a time in my life when I finally understand the feminine nature. The experience has made me a crone, a wise one, a traveled pilgrim who has trod the road of life for many years. I have learned vital lessons, cried in pain through births, laughed with joy at baby's first steps, anguished over lost loves, delighted over new loves, and skated along the icy path of life.

I realize that despite the richness of my life no one ever told me I could do anything I wanted, and no one said it would be easy. I also was never told that my creativity could make all the difference in how I perceived and enjoyed life.

Raised in a strict, sometimes violent Italian home, I learned to disappear at appropriate times, study hard, and isolate myself with numerous (but hardly age-appropriate) chores around the house, all to prove I was worthy of being a child in my parents' home. I created a life of my own, as I secretly wished I were someone else, somewhere else, prettier, smarter, indestructible.

At around age 12, I arrived late at my father's small grocery store because of an error in timing. My father, enraged, sent me down to the dark basement and shut the door. At first, I just sat there, fearful and puzzled, wondering why my mother allowed my father to treat me this way. But, as the hours passed, my thoughts changed, and I discovered that they led me on a journey into creativity. I sang, made up stories, and listened as the heels of the people overhead clicked over the grating. I made up names for my imaginary friends. By the time I was finally let up into the store, I had resolved to never again be in fear and always to use my brains and courage to my best advantage. It was a transformative moment.

From then on, through Catholic high school and college, I was in a state of constant creativity. I used my creative spirit to keep out of trouble with the nuns, and I played piano loudly enough at home to drown out the constant arguing. I imagined the darkness away through creative activities and shared these sparks of inspiration with my little brother, who was someone I protected when the "action" started.

When I was older and began to have children, I used my creative abilities again – not only as I engaged the feelings of what it meant to have lives entrusted to me – but also literally, through the creation process of birth. But, when I was nine months pregnant with my fourth baby, the life within me stopped.

"You are carrying a non-viable fetus," the doctors told me, with the instructions to go home and wait. I went home, waited, and delivered my child – in the bed where we had created him – and wept. Since the baby was still in a "cocoon," I did not know until weeks later that I had delivered a son. Then, I wept again. For the first time since I'd discovered my creative juices, they seemed to be dried up.

I knew I once again had to launch the life force that would bring back my spirit, the life force that I knew beat within me. It took time for me to rejuvenate mentally, emotionally, and physically, but two years later, I birthed a beautiful, smiling baby girl into the world. It felt like a rebirth of my own creative spirit!

When my children were older, I allowed my creative juices to swim into a deep pool of the unknown when I returned to college. I had received a full scholarship to college after high school but had left after two years to focus on my home life. Through the years, my heart and soul had yearned to finish my degree, and, finally, I had an opportunity to return.

With the encouragement of my late husband, there I was, 48 years old, with a backpack. It was an entirely new journey of creativity. I majored in drama, art, and women's studies, and traveled to Brazil and China to complete a paper on women's lives and experiences. I taught fellow students the finer points of Italian before a trip to Italy to study the art and sculpture of the Renaissance. My creativity was bursting at my seams! All those years with my creativity focused in other directions, and I was finally realizing how much I had inside for myself! It is said that when we follow our joy, our success will fall in line, and this proved true with the amazing energy I felt and the resulting accolades – twice I appeared on the Dean's list and earned the title of Valedictorian.

While studying, I also discovered a love for sculpture and painting, inclinations I'd never recognized before. Creating a soaring eagle from what had been only a block of green granite fulfilled a need so primitive to my soul that I can never go back! I now feel I must always be creating. I see things so differently, so much larger, and pulsating with energy. I often find myself rushing to my studio, a new idea bursting forth before I can even arrive and pick up my brushes.

How have I not given up, despite all the ruts in the road, the brambles scratching my legs, the sorrows and disappointments that constantly appeared? I will tell you why … because as women we have the stamina, faith, and sheer will to survive that, coupled with creativity, brings forth for our sisters a beacon to follow when dark times come around.

I truly believe that my childhood experiences, combined with my own process of birthing children, made me stronger, more willful and energetic, and more able to access the feminine spirit – this invisible force that allows us to pull out our innermost strength to constantly and courageously be creative for one and all, including ourselves.

How amazing is this creative feminine energy we have. It keeps on giving and giving and giving. If only we respect and accept and rejoice in its giving! I believe we are constant students, and as women, we give and receive to each other on a daily basis, reaching for those behind us, receiving a hand from those ahead of us.

Just before I was born, women finally received the right to vote. Can you believe it? I walk on the shoulders of so many of the feminine, the brave, and the fearless. I am so thankful. When I speak to women's groups, I hope I pass on the message to "Always Remember." The paths were paved for us, and now we must repave the road for our younger sisters … for those who still need to discover their own creative energies. Globally, women all desire the same things – peace for our families, a safe place to live, food on our tables, and a loving atmosphere in which to create.

The older I get, the more I am able to pull deep down into that space of the feminine energy and constantly create what is within. My muse has entered its senior time. The time when, I was once told, life should be quiescent, slow, a "looking back and remembering" time.

Not I! This is the most invigorating part of my life! A time when I am becoming more creative and more eager to learn. This is when I read great books, write the book I have been working on mentally for over ten years, enjoy the fruits of my labors, and laugh at the things I thought were so serious in the past. When I think about the wasted days worrying about things that never happened, ignoring the feminine spirit that was brewing just beneath the surface ...

Now, toward the end of the runway, I am surprised by the strength and vigor and insistence of the creative force that constantly awakens in me! As I look back over the life I have experienced, I sing with joy!

....

Carmel Rivello Maguire influenced design for over 25 years as founder of Carmelot Interiors, Inc. and as executive vice president of strategic planning and business development for two major interior design firms specializing in hotel and resort/hospitality design in California and Florida. She is one of the first women to be invited to join Rotary International in the San Fernando Valley, California area; one of the first women in the country to be elected "Rotarian of the Year;" and is the recipient of a Paul Harris Fellow award. During her time in hospitality design, she became a much sought-after industry speaker in the United States, Mexico, the Bahamas, and Hawaii. She also was a frequent contributor to "Developments Magazine," one of the resort industry's premiere international publications.

Carmel is living proof that thirst for knowledge never ends. Carmel returned to college later in life at California Lutheran University to complete her degree. Next to her love of family, Carmel's passions include gardening, sculpting, and Italian cooking. Her service efforts include working to refurbish a non-profit treatment and transitional women's center in Ventura County, California. She brings the work of her late husband Frank Maguire forward and is a much sought-after humorist speaker.

Quest for Beauty

By Beverly Solomon, creative director for musee-solomon

....

Do you remember reading stories where the heroine was both bright and beautiful? Probably not, but – despite what many would try to tell you – being that woman is possible.

I was fortunate to have been born to a beautiful and creative mother. She was a fashion designer in Miami in the late 1940s and early 1950s, and, as a child, I would look at her design sketches and dream about wearing beautiful clothes to beautiful places. I would take naps in my mother's closet and look up at her beautiful chiffon dresses in a variety of colors like lilac, sea green, and sunshine yellow. The colors looked like melting popsicles over my head.

My mother loved art and would tell me stories about her favorite artists. By the time I entered kindergarten, I knew all of the major impressionists. I loved telling the story about Vincent Van Gogh, who cut his ear off for his "girlfriend." Every summer, my mother sent me to art classes sponsored by the museum. This enhanced my love and appreciation for art. As I grew older, she also sent me to "charm school" to polish my social skills.

With my fashion background, I started modeling for local, upscale department stores at 15. By 16, I was working in a cosmetic department. I was making fun money, learning business, and meeting interesting and creative people. Because I dressed stylishly and looked and acted older than I was, I often was invited to society parties and functions where influential women shared advice on both love and business. I used my money wisely and avoided many of the pitfalls of the teenage years.

Unfortunately, I also was becoming physically weaker. It seemed my life was one continuous menstrual cycle. After years of uncertainty, I finally was diagnosed with cervical cancer caused by DES, a drug – designed to prevent miscarriage – that was given to my mother while she was pregnant with me. At only 18, I was told that to save my life, I would need to have a hysterectomy.

As one can imagine, I had to deal with a wide range of emotions. However, I was more calm and confident about my upcoming surgery than most of the adults that surrounded me. I was extremely fortunate to have had a doctor who assured me he would do all he could to make me cancer free. Somehow, I knew everything would be all right.

After my surgery, which was considered a success, I felt great and was raring to go again. I immediately gained weight and was thrilled when I made it to a hundred pounds. I felt good and saw my doctor once a month for check-ups.

Nine months later, my doctor found more cancer cells. He explained to me that there were a few cells so small they were missed the first time around but had now grown bigger. He wanted to cut them out immediately before they spread. As much as I trusted my doctor, I was scared this time. Again, my surgery was considered a success, but I wasn't sure. The people who had been there for me nine months before were not with me this time. My mother was the only person who visited me in the hospital. No one seemed close to me, and I started to feel isolated. For the first time in my life, I felt depressed.

One Sunday morning, I woke up and decided to go for a drive to clear my head. I had a '72 Olds Cutlass Supreme convertible. I had the top down and was cruising around town. I drove by my old church and decided to stop in. I sat down in the back pew and began to pray with all my heart and soul. Suddenly, I felt washed with warmth, and I felt like I was floating on a cloud. I was unbelievably happy. I left the church knowing I had plans to make for my life.

Unlike other young women of my age who were going to college, enjoying their freedom, and dreaming of meeting Prince Charming, I didn't know what the future held for me so I decided to become serious about my health, life, and goals. Since my love for fashion and beauty was in my blood, I sought a job working for the best in the industry. Luckily, Diane von Furstenberg, a woman I admired as a designer, a business woman, and a person, gave me my first big break. I helped launch her first fragrance, "Tatiana," in the 1970s. I also had the privilege of working with von Furstenberg at trunk shows and book signings. She was a creative business woman making money, yet she celebrated her femininity. She created an empire encouraging other women to be feminine and powerful at the same time. She was a great role model, and I tried to pattern myself after her.

I eventually worked as an account executive in sales and marketing for a number of outstanding companies in the fashion and beauty industry – including Revlon and Ralph Lauren. I am proud to say I became one of the top salespeople in the nation and still maintained my femininity and morals. But, it was not always easy to do!

The fashion and beauty business was a male-dominated industry in the 1970s and 1980s. A woman was too often promoted only after supplying her boss with sex and/or drugs. I chose to stick to my principles. At the time, many people equated being feminine, polite, and caring with weakness. I learned to use that underestimation to my advantage. While some of my colleagues were in and out of rehab and dysfunctional relationships, I kept my focus on business opportunities and saving money for my life goals.

As my health improved, not only did I advance my career goals, but I also kept up my interest in art. I met my husband, internationally-recognized artist Pablo Solomon, at an art show while buying some of his work. At that time, artists were copying Andy Warhol and other contemporary artists. I was bored with the same predictable art at every show I attended. Pablo's art caught my eye first because it was black and white and also because the subject was people portraying emotions. It touched me in a very powerful way. When we met, it was love at first sight for both of us.

When Pablo proposed to me, I said yes, but I had to tell him I couldn't have children. I was afraid this would be a deal breaker. I was relieved when he told me he loved me and that if we felt a need for children, we would adopt. We were married two months later and have now been happily married for over three decades. We never adopted children, but we have worked with children's charities, rescued animals, and worked on environmental issues. Through these activities, I feel thoroughly satisfied as a woman.

Although I experienced success in the corporate world, I wanted to be my own boss. I also wanted the opportunity to use my experience, knowledge, and connections to promote Pablo's art and visionary environmental designs. After one of my bosses and I had a knock-down, drag-out fight because I told him he needed to put more time into the business and less time into drugs and personal messes, I decided it was time to go out on my own. I opened my own art and design business, which primarily focused on Pablo's work.

After years of using my sales and marketing skills, I have made Pablo one of the most recognized artists in the world. In art, name recognition is everything. Pablo has appeared in over 20 books, dozens of major magazines and newspapers, been on national television and international radio, and was even the subject of a short film on HBO. While Pablo can take credit for his great art and design work, I can say I made him the most recognized "Pablo" in art since Picasso.

Through hard work, discipline, shared goals, and tenacity, Pablo and I have created a wonderful life on our historic 1856 ranch in the beautiful Texas Hill Country north of Austin. Our ranch is not only a state historic site and an official Texas Wildscape but also has been nominated for the highest award in Texas for land stewardship. We're very fortunate to be able to divide our time between living on our beautiful ranch and promoting Pablo's art in the great cities around the world. I feel proud and fulfilled by my path of feminine growth. And, yes, I do all this while wearing beautiful clothes!

. . . .

Beverly Solomon is currently creative director for musee-solomon. She was a model and then an account executive in sales and marketing for Diane von Furstenberg, Revlon, and Ralph Lauren. She now lives and works with her husband, internationally-recognized artist Pablo Solomon, on their 1856 historic ranch in the Texas Hill Country north of Austin. She manages their art and design business and also provides expertise in the areas of art, fashion, and beauty. She has been featured in books, newspapers, magazines, and television. Beverly has received coverage in a number of financial publications and was given official recognition by the State of Texas for her business savvy. You can visit her at www.beverlysolomon.com.

I am Creative.

1. I play for at least a few minutes every day.

2. I gift myself with true freedom in my thoughts and in my actions.

3. I imagine how I would like to be – and picture that I already am so.

4. I create through dancing, painting, writing, cooking – whatever free-form activities I enjoy exploring.

5. I recognize that creation is about the experience, not the outcome.

intuition

Hildegard of Bingen

"A human being is a vessel that God has built for himself and filled with his inspiration so that his works are perfected in it." – Hildegard of Bingen, Letter to Elisabeth of Schönau, c. 1152

Hildegard of Bingen recorded her intricate visions in text, art, and music, which communicated emotion and philosophy across continents and centuries.

....

In 1098, at the time of her birth, Hildegard of Bingen, the tenth child of a noble family in Nahe, Germany, was dedicated to the church as a traditional tithe. Large numbers of children were difficult to care for and feed, and the dedications were a common practice of the time. At eight years old, Hildegard was sent to study with an anchoress at Mount St. Disibode. She studied Latin and learned biblical verse. At age 18, she became a nun. Twenty years later, at age 38, she became head of the female members of the Benedictine monastery.

In 1141, Hildegard experienced a vision that changed her life: she saw God give her an instantaneous understanding of religious texts. He then commanded her to record everything she saw in her recurring visions. She described the experience, writing, "And it came to pass . . . when I was 42 years and seven months old, that the heavens were opened and a blinding light of exceptional brilliance flowed through my entire brain. And so it kindled my whole heart and breast like a flame, not burning but warming . . . and suddenly I understood the meaning of expositions of the books."

Despite the vision, self-doubt plagued Hildegard. "Because of low opinion of myself and because of diverse sayings of men, I refused for a long time a call to write, not out of stubbornness but out of humility, until weighed down by a scourge of God, I fell onto a bed of sickness," she wrote.

Eventually, Hildegard answered the call to share her visions and dreams, and she sought verification by the Catholic Church that what she saw had divine origins. With aid from St. Bernard, Hildegard's writing and drawings were shown to Pope Eugenius. With his encouragement, she finished her first work, *Scivias*, "Know the Way(s of the Lord)," and gained a reputation throughout Germany.

In 1150, Hildegard reestablished her convent along the banks of the Rhine in Bingen, to accommodate a growing number of nuns. There, her fame grew as she continued recording her divine visions as ornate illustrations and text. She also gained fame for composing beautiful liturgical music and lyrics that honored the saints and Mary, and proclaimed the potential of every human and the necessity of social justice. In her music, Hildegard explored themes concerning humanity's place in divine creation. Her natural writings, two books known together as Liber subtilatum, "The Book of Subtleties of the Diverse Nature of Things," were based on her philosophy that humans were the pinnacle of divine creation.

Hildegard also was a pioneer in the fields of horticulture and medicine; she researched the potential of plants to cure pain and disease. Scientists are revisiting her work today, and reinvigorating her legacy. She also traveled extensively throughout Germany, Switzerland, and France, where she delivered deeply moving sermons that grew her popularity. She passed away on September 17, 1179.

. . . .

- Recognized by Rome as a religious authority at a time when women had little influence
- Wrote and performed Christian musical plays that have been reproduced today
- Experienced visions that enlightened her theology and led her to create beautiful documentation of the images she saw and words she heard
- Fused religion, science, and art in her body of work

Saint Teresa of Avila

"The soul is a castle made entirely out of a diamond or a very clear crystal, in which there are many rooms." – Saint Teresa of Ávila

St. Teresa of Ávila, while incredibly active on an earthly level, remains most known for her inner spiritual journey and the cataloguing of this journey through her many writings.

....

St. Teresa, also known as Saint Teresa of Jesus, was a prominent Spanish mystic born in 1515. As a child, she was fascinated by adventure stories of quests for the Holy Grail and dreamed of performing knightly deeds. She also was intent on martyrdom among the Moors, and she once ran away from home – only to be discovered by an uncle just as she reached the exterior walls of her city. Well known for her playful spirit, valiant heart, and strong will to be true to herself, Teresa was popular and enjoyed her friends and potential suitors. However, she feared marriage because of how it enslaved women in her time, and – at the age of 20 – escaped again. She entered into a Carmelite convent in secret.

As an adult, Teresa suffered a severe bout of malaria. Four days after she had experienced a seizure, Teresa woke up to learn others had dug a grave for her. She remained paralyzed for three years and suffered a great deal of pain. Never completely well, Teresa used her poor health as a reason to stop praying for a period of time. Eventually, she resumed the act of prayer and found that she was finally able to connect in an intimate way with God.

From within her "Interior Castle," Teresa experienced moments of spiritual ecstasy. She also saw and spoke with God, Jesus, angels, and other spiritual beings, levitated during Mass and in the convent, and experienced her heart being pierced by the lance of an angel. Critics described these experiences as from the devil, and this caused Teresa great distress, to the point that she injured herself intentionally.

Through her many writings, she focuses on the inner journey for peace and self-contemplation and compares mystical prayer to watering a garden. Her books include: her autobiography, "The Life of Teresa of Jesus;" "El Castillo Interior (The Interior Castle;)" and "Camino de Perfección (The Way of Perfection.)" Teresa died in 1582. October 15 is her feast day in the Catholic faith.

- Founded the Discalced Carmelites, with the assistance of fellow mystic, John of the Cross
- Beatified in 1614
- Canonized by Pope Gregory XV in 1622
- Declared the first woman Doctor of the Church by Paul VI in 1970

Essays By Women

Awakening Feminine Intuition with Guided Imagery

By Leslie Davenport, author of "Healing and Transformation Through Self-Guided Imagery" and founding member of the Institute for Health & Healing in San Francisco, California

....

Right now, everyone on earth is hurtling through space at 19 miles per second on a mud ball. When you stop to think about it, that is an absolutely awe-inspiring fact. And, it's one that only leads to more questions. What is this place? Why are we here?

Science investigates such questions; religions contemplate; the arts find fresh ways to express wonder. But, the answers proclaimed by any discipline continually shift and change with time. Each theory launches a flurry of questions that peels back layers and layers of unknowing.

And yet, here we are, in the midst of it all, able to ask these questions, as rare and mysterious humans – beings filled with consciousness, surrounded by a seemingly endless array of vibrant minerals, plants, and animals. Rather than being a problem to be solved, we can view not-knowing as a gift that calls us into grateful living. Not-knowing is a way of cultivating intuition – a way that is available to every person who lets go of preconceived notions and opens to the feminine aspect of receptivity. Not-knowing opens the eyes of the heart to see us as the living miracles we are.

Seeing with the eyes of the heart can be developed with a practice known as guided imagery. Guided imagery is a method of heightening self-awareness to the subtle workings of our body/mind/emotions/spirit, which reveal themselves to us through images. It shifts our feminine receptivity into the foreground. As we become familiar with our own inner landscapes, we understand how the many facets of ourselves are intimately connected and how they influence each other and the world around us.

For example, if our awareness is present to our essential, vibrant aliveness, it helps us appreciate the simple miracles in daily life: healthy food, friendships, the beauty of a sunset. Conversely, if we are wrapped up in worry, the world is small, dismal, and scary. Fear-based images release a cascade of stress chemicals in the body. Stressed, we're less available in our relationships, our decisions are fueled by anxiety, and the day slips by in a blur.

Imagery practice has ancient roots and is a very natural way of knowing ourselves and life. But, it has been severely underutilized in our contemporary culture where the more masculine aspects of achievement, analysis, and organization are prized. While logic is necessary and valuable, when we fail to draw upon the full range of human capacity, it creates imbalance. The cumulative lack of balance eventually becomes unsustainable, which leads to the environmental, economic, and health crises we're now seeing on a global scale. It is vital that we ask ourselves how we got here and that we embrace the diminished feminine aspects of our humanity to correct the imbalance. As Einstein said, "Problems cannot be solved by the same consciousness that created them."

I'm not suggesting that had we all done imagery, these problems would not exist, but I am saying that we have collectively lost sight of the mystery, beauty, and soulful aspects of life. Imagery is a powerful way to remain connected with the deep aspects of life that emerge though the feminine side of our consciousness.

I was a professional modern dancer before I entered psychology, and that is where I first learned how to balance our feminine, intuitive nature with our masculine, structured side. I experienced the rigorous technical precision of dance as the masculine component of the art form, and the creative inspiration as that which arose from feminine receptivity. It took focused effort to master the rigors of dance technique, but I had to let go completely to access the creativity.

For years, I explored how my body could be a receptive vessel to emotions and qualities, and I gave it free reign of expression. What was I feeling that caused my body to slump to the floor in an asymmetrical heap, or run in spirals with arms wide open? If I embodied certain postures, I noticed that I had flashes of insight about life and about myself – my feelings and perspectives shifted. While I was pleased that I could design and make movements happen, I was much more intrigued by what moved me!

When the more masculine precision of dance technique blends with the creative feminine flow of expression, dance becomes living images infused with power and inspiration. It is in the synthesis of the masculine and feminine aspects that the movement gains richness, clarity, depth, and vibrancy. And, so, too, with balance in our lives!

Because dance engages the networks connecting our thoughts, emotions, spirit, and physiology, it gradually led me to explore the healing aspects of creativity and images. I knew firsthand that wisdom-based images constantly arise within us. What would happen if we accessed these images as clues for healing? I found out by creating guided imagery programs within hospitals.

Roselyn, a petite and energetic woman in her early forties, came into my therapy practice to try guided imagery after she had undergone a lumpectomy for breast cancer. She was about to begin radiation treatment. Because she came from a hard hitting, achievement-driven profession, she had set out to bulldoze her cancer with the same force of will that had served her career.

Equipped with a large, leather briefcase packed with her recent research on cancer, she briskly handed me three articles on the benefits of guided imagery. After having briefed herself on how lymphocytes and antibodies work in the blood stream, she aimed to buzz through her cancer treatment and beef up her T-cells and B-cells without missing a beat. She planned to get her immune system to shape up and to get her cancer under control.

Roselyn had prepared to do "directed" imagery, a masculine, take-charge, "mind over matter" approach. In "directed" sessions, you picture how your body or another part of you "ought" to be functioning, and install the correct images via a script. While that imagery method can be useful, it's a one-size-fits-all approach, and, well, we're not all one size. Non-scripted imagery evokes our feminine receptive side. Through it, we learn to listen, see, and sense what we may need at any particular time. We then explore the unique images that arise from within us, drawing upon resources from our body/mind/emotions/spirit. I suggested we try receptive imagery, and Roselyn agreed. What came through her imagery, as her focus shifted from her head to her heart, caught her completely by surprise.

At the beginning of our imagery, I invited Roselyn to close her eyes and settle back in the reclining chair. I guided her through a breathing exercise and progressive relaxation, continuing until I saw that she was comfortable and at ease. I encouraged Roselyn to simply be receptive to any image that arose that could represent her own well-functioning immune system and let her know it could come in any form.

"When an image appears, whether or not it even makes sense to you," I encouraged, "go ahead and describe it aloud."

After a short pause, she began:

"I'm ten, maybe eleven, standing in the patio of my parents' home. I can still smell the barbequed sausage that we just had for dinner. It's warm outside and quiet."

With her eyes still closed and her brows pinched together, she looked curious and surprised. "Sheba, my tabby cat, is here. She is beginning to give birth to a litter of kittens. I crouch down by her side, but feel panicky in my stomach. What should I do to help her? What if something goes wrong? My parents are down the street at a neighbor's house, and I'm by myself."

While I didn't know what this had to do with her immune health, I trusted the process and stayed with it. "What happens next?" I asked.

"Sheba looks up at me, and I just stay by her side. It seems like she really, really wants me here."

We paused again together, joined in the anticipation of the moment.

"Wow! I see that she knows exactly what to do." She tilted her head to the side and squinted, though her eyes remained closed. Soon, a smile spread across her face. "The kittens launch into the world, absolutely perfect and healthy. Sheba cleans them, nurtures them. It's so simple and so natural."

The imagery session continued a few minutes, and Roselyn lingered in the awe of the birth. When she opened her eyes, her face was soft and open; her eyes shone. She spoke much more slowly and looked directly into my eyes.

"I had it backwards. Sheba showed me that she didn't 'make it happen.' She somehow participated in something much bigger than herself. And, it no longer makes sense to take charge of my blood cells in the way I was thinking about it before."

We both paused to take in the profound beauty of her new-found perspective. Roselyn's eyes welled up with tears, and she reached for a tissue.

"I know what I have to do," she stated with strength and conviction. "I want to stand by my side, the way I stood by Sheba. I see how I've bullied myself, running on coffee and sweets into 14-hour days. For maybe the first time in my life, I want to be a good friend to myself."

A jumble of shame and relief poured out of Roselyn, as a new view of herself dawned. She described many ways her high-pressure life had put her out of touch with her body's natural rhythms. Reviving Roselyn's feminine nature launched her own rebirth into a new way of being.

Being a witness to Roselyn's journey left me filled with gratitude and helped me remember the wondrous generosity of life itself, even in the midst of very difficult circumstances. Yet, it is important to remember that Roselyn's story is just one example of the transformative power of feminine receptivity that is available to us all, men and women. While the shape of our lives may be worlds apart from Roselyn's, our receptive feminine is here to guide and support us – whether in the midst of a current crisis, reflecting on a significant life transition, or simply deepening gratitude in day-to-day moments. Witnessing her path was an invitation, a reminder that the doorway to wisdom within stands open.

To experience the transformative power of your own feminine receptivity, try this simple imagery practice:

When you have about 20 minutes of undisturbed time, sit or recline in a comfortable way, and close your eyes. Take three to five minutes to simply breathe as though you could inhale and exhale though your emotional/spiritual heart. Imagine the breath as it enters and exits through a window in your heart that's open to a warm breeze. Every time you exhale, release tension in your body, and let go of thoughts. When you inhale, simply enjoy the freshness and calmness of your breath, and let your inner gaze rest in your heart.

When you are feeling relaxed, invite an image to form for any message your heart has for you right now. It may appear as a symbol, a color, a word, or even just a felt sense. You could bring a specific question or concern to your heart, or just notice whatever rises in the moment. Allow the image to have a voice, and be open to however it expresses itself to you.

Thank your heart, and be present to the feelings and wisdom that linger, and gently open your eyes.

May you go into the world with your intuition and sharp reasoning fully integrated and accessible. May you give and receive, speak and listen, inspire and respond, and walk in wisdom and in love.

....

Leslie Davenport has unique qualifications in the body-mind-spirit field. Dance critic Allan Ulrich reviewed Leslie as a professional dancer endowed with "a superior sense of balance … and powers of communication that set her apart from the herd." As a psychotherapist in practice for twenty years, she understands the health impact of thoughts and emotions, and a passion for the mystery of the human spirit drew her to become an ordained interfaith minister in 1984. Leslie has braided her expertise with body-mind-spirit into her book, "Healing and Transformation Through Self-Guided Imagery."

Leslie is a founding member of the Institute for Health & Healing at California Pacific Medical Center in San Francisco, which brings holistic care into the heart of conventional medicine. She is on faculty at John F. Kennedy University, and she is clinical supervisor for the California Institute of Integral Studies. A sought-after speaker and consultant, Leslie lectures in a broad range of settings that have included KRON Television, the National Wellness Conference, Rancho La Puerta, and Commonwealth Club. For more information, visit www.LeslieDavenport.com.

Coming to America

By Elizabeth Harper, author of "Wishing: How to Fulfill Your Heart's Desires," founder of Sealed With Love LLC, and co-founder of Spiritual Living LLC

....

I twice shunned wedded bliss. When I was seventeen years old, my would-be fiancé left for university, and I soon came to the realization that life without him was more fun than life with him. My next near-miss came when my Greek business partner and part-time boyfriend thought an offer of marriage would make me stay put. Much to his chagrin, it had the opposite effect. Marriage was a fine institution; it just wasn't for me – at least that had always been my stand. The truth was, at the age of 37, I felt alone.

One day, as I sat in a friend's kitchen, I exclaimed I had a "feeling" urging me to visit the United States. My friend did not doubt my words; he simply asked, "Why?" Usually, such a question would prime my intuitive circuitry to generate a response, but in this instance I didn't have an answer.

This was out of character for me; I always had an answer! I had no particular desire to see America, yet I yearned to be there. The feeling persisted, pushing me to make a move. I attempted to ignore it, thinking it would go away, but it didn't.

My intuition told me I had to go to New York, even though I believed California to be more in line with who I was. It was in the very nature of my being to want to know more. Why did I need to visit the U.S. and why New York? Ordinarily, I gained access to intuitive information by handling it like a search engine – I would ask a question and the answer would come. But, it didn't work. The answer continued to evade me, and so I consulted a psychic in the hope of receiving some clarity.

The psychic I chose came highly recommended by a friend. Her claim to fame was that Princess Diana had consulted with her. In my session, she offered me advice that was in conflict with what I felt. She told me I would never visit the U.S. I was confused by her remarks, especially as my feelings told me otherwise. It became a good lesson for me to trust my own self and my own intuition. I wondered what the Princess had been told, and if she, too, had needed clarity on an intuitive feeling.

It was the late 1990s, and a friend introduced me to the Internet. Through this wonderful tool, I corresponded with two pen pals, one in New York and the other in New Jersey. They felt like my guardian angels. Both agreed to let me stay with them, sight unseen. However, my friends in London, because of their own fears, tried to persuade me to stay in England. One told me it was dangerous to stay with people I didn't know, but he found it hard to trust and was suspicious of everyone. Another advised me that it was time to settle down, buy a house, and make roots, but it was she who needed this kind of security to feel safe. I had spent my life with the wind blowing through my hair, and I was determined to follow my heart fearlessly. It had always steered me in the right direction, and I wasn't about to give up on it now.

It had been two years since the feelings began, and every day they grew stronger. I weighed my choices: I could take a leap of faith and follow my intuition or forever numb my feelings and be prepared for the consequences. I bought a plane ticket and left England on an adventure.

As soon as the plane landed at JFK International Airport in New York, I felt like I had come home. The wheels touched the ground, and my heart filled with joy – I knew I was exactly where I was supposed to be. Despite extensive travel, I had always felt like a nomad in search of the perfect place to pitch a tent. Every place I had lived, I felt like a square peg in a round hole. Now, for the first time in my life, I had found the place for which my heart had been searching.

There was, however, one insurmountable obstacle to fulfilling my heart's desire: I was British. Unless I offered a unique qualification, was an Olympic world record holder or Nobel Prize winner, or came from Irish stock, I could not legally remain in the U.S. for any extended length of time. I needed a miracle – but first I made a wish!

Some wishes manifest as a result of clear vision so, to help myself focus, I compiled two lists – a career plan and a man plan. They were specific to my needs and united the most important aspects of my life. My career plan embraced my desire to live in a healing community that offered teaching spaces with wooden floors, big windows, lots of flowers, and an abundance of throw cushions. I envisioned a country setting with wooden chalets for people to stay in and flowing water nearby. My man plan was less detailed: I wanted someone with strong character who would know me inside and out. He would accept me for who I was, he would have the freedom to travel, and, most importantly, he would be available.

Shortly after devising my plans, I picked up a copy of a magazine and noticed an advertisement for seasonal staff at a holistic community called Omega. Nestled in the woods in upstate New York, Omega (the largest holistic center in North America) caters to the mind, body, and spirit of those seeking enlightenment. Workshops are conducted in wooden buildings with a profusion of throw cushions. Participants stay in chalets surrounded by nature and an array of water features. It ticked every one of my career-plan boxes. I arranged to work as a volunteer and returned at the beginning of the work season. A silver-haired man greeted me in Omega's parking lot on my first day. It was love at first sight – I was two for two!

Our friendship deepened and soon developed into a loving partnership. I was surprised by how quickly we became attached to one another. He made me feel nurtured and loved, and he touched my heart in a way I had not experienced before. On the one hand, our bond was exhilarating, and, on the other, it brought up a fear of loss. This is the relationship I had longed for, however, and I was prepared to do whatever it took to keep our love for one another on course. I still had clients and teaching commitments back in England so I traveled back and forth, but I missed him and my newfound home desperately.

In May 2000, the start of the second year of our relationship, I had a strong feeling to remain in the U.S. and not return to England until autumn. This would automatically revoke my tourist visa. Despite the anticipated penalty, I followed my feelings and trusted that everything would work out for my highest good. Staying in one place gave me the opportunity to write a book and, at the same time, establish a deeper connection with my boyfriend. On my return to England, I had an intuitive feeling that something big was going to happen to change the course of my life, and it would occur around Christmas. I fantasized that my book would be published. I would emerge a huge star and be welcomed back into the U.S. as an honorary citizen. It would soon become clear that this could not be farther from the truth!

I had never spent Christmas in the U.S. before, and I was excited at the prospect. I got a direct flight from London to Charlotte, North Carolina, where I would meet my boyfriend's family. As the plane came in to land, I looked out of my window and wondered why I couldn't imagine myself driving along the roads. Something was wrong, and the answer was painful: I was denied entry to the U.S. I had been a bad girl and overstayed my tourist visa. In my naiveté, I had expected the immigration authorities to slap me on my hands and tell me not to do it again. Instead, I was searched, interrogated, and then marched onto an airplane back to England with the words, "From now on, you have to apply for a regular visa" ringing in my ears. Two officers escorted me to my gate while my boyfriend watched, speechless. A former U.S. Marine who had fought for his country and received a Purple Heart for his courage, he now felt powerless to fight for his love. Once he recovered his composure, he boarded the next flight to England and joined me in London for the holidays.

We got married at Bethesda Naval Hospital in Washington, D.C., just over a year later. My book, "Wishing: How to Fulfill Your Heart's Desires," was published in 2008, eight years after it was written. Some might say it took too long for my dreams to come to fruition, but I firmly believe that everything has its own perfect timing. My book came out exactly when it needed to – when the economy was suffering. I came to the U.S. and met my boyfriend at the exact moment he was available. That first leap of faith took me on a journey that changed every aspect of my life. Had I not followed my feelings, I marvel at how my life would have differed. Would I have written a book, married a soul mate, created two successful businesses, built my own home, and become an American citizen? I doubt it.

As children, we unknowingly catch glimpses of the fabric of our future. My brother recently reminded me that as a child I'd told him I would live in the U.S. I have no recollection of my prophetic statement and had not thought to catalogue my predictions. I question what other gems of wisdom rolled off my tongue, only to be lost!

It is my belief that we are in partnership with a Divine intelligence, one that guides us to achieve our highest purpose. This intelligence has a number of names: God, Goddess, Spirit, Jehovah, etc. I call it Great Spirit, perhaps because my mother used this expression. I was fortunate to have been raised in an environment where philosophical discussions, intuitive insights, and psychic feelings where considered the norm. My mother was one of the pioneers of yoga in Britain; to her, yoga was a way of life, and yogi philosophies were at the heart of all other truth-seeking works.

My intuition was empowered by her belief that this dominant force was a natural part of every woman's make-up and was not to be disregarded nor dishonored. I was encouraged to nurture my insatiable appetite for knowledge, and over time, I naturally gained insight into the individual expression of my intuitive gifts. Everything I learned in childhood from my amazing mother and from books is the source of my teaching and work today.

I have learned that when we listen to our intuition and follow our feelings, we are being guided by the best GPS system in existence – our souls. Our heart is the voice of our soul, and our feelings convey its messages. Trust that in any given moment the gentle whispers of the sleeping Goddess within you will reveal the right course of action for your highest good. All we have to do is listen. Occasionally, you'll be inspired to take a leap of faith, and even though your friends might insist you would be crazy to take the leap, remember that your soul is directing you to take the journey. Your friends have their own GPS systems. Trust in yours.

. . . .

Elizabeth Harper is a popular and inspiring teacher, color intuitive, and psychic artist who empowers others to realize their light. The award-winning author of "Wishing: How to Fulfill Your Heart's Desires," she has been featured in popular national magazines, including Woman's World, Redbook, Prevention, and Health. She also is a magazine columnist and regular contributor to radio and television in the U.S. and Australia. Her pioneering work with color inspired her uniquely revealing ColorScope, featured globally in print and online magazines. Elizabeth shares her gift of healing with color through her visionary jewelry, Silk Energy Wraps, and personal creations. She is the founder of Sealed With Love LLC and co-founder of Spiritual Living LLC, an online education center. www.sealedwithlove.com

The Secret Place of the Most High

By Gayle Newhouse, co-producer of "Tapping the Source"

. . . .

By the time I was three years old, my mother knew my touch could calm and heal. She and I would spend time alone together, lying on her bed, and she would generously share her jewels. Oh, how I loved going through her jewelry box! She would ask for my touch, and I would lightly lay my hands over her, rejuvenating her body for the evening ahead. When my mother had a headache or was tired, she would lie on the bed and ask me to touch her back or neck. Though this was not a conventional practice in those days, she knew I could change her energy and restore wellbeing with a simple touch.

At five years old, going to bed – leaving the physical plane and dancing with the energies of the Universe – became my fondest part of the day. I remember, as clearly as yesterday, an inner voice telling me that I "could dance with the energies but was never to touch any fields that were not mine." Obediently, I complied.

By seven, I was seeing and conversing with angelic beings. My sensitivity became overwhelming; it pierced the veil very acutely and often. I often cried for what I understood to be heaven – I wanted so badly to go back home to the Light I loved. But the angels did not listen to my pleas, and I awoke breathing, disappointed, and still in bed on earth.

Somehow, I had a powerful knowledge that to survive on this planet would require me to understand the dark side of human nature. I knew innocence and humanity didn't go well hand in hand, and I loved my freedom to be innocent. As I grew up, I could feel the threats to my innocence, and I grew angry with God. I couldn't realize until much later in life how important the intense disappointment of those times was to becoming a strong, powerful, healthy, loving woman.

Learning anger and to control my disappointments had advantages. Once, earlier in my childhood, I had brutally attacked a neighbor one block over, and then run for my life – straight into my bedroom. Then, the doorbell rang. I anxiously held my breath, as I desperately hoped the visitor would go away. No such luck.

My father sternly called me to the door to meet a very large, 12-year-old boy with a bloody nose and the boy's furious father. I was shaking. Tommy was the neighborhood bully, but he especially enjoyed chasing after younger kids like me and would threaten to hurt us. My father always insisted that I stand up for myself and what was right, so I did. I punched him in the nose and knocked him down.

Tommy's father took one look at my petite, eight-year-old self, and his anger shifted from me to his son. Embarrassed, he grabbed Tommy by the ear and stomped off while my father chuckled. I had escaped punishment;

my father's eyes looked into mine with pride, and I knew another bully was off the streets. This sagacious moment empowered my intuitive side, which felt this act of violence was somehow righteous and would somehow save Tommy a life of dissension.

As a teen, I learned how to survive as a female in a male-dominated world. My dear father, bless his confused heart, was subjected to a strong-willed, teenage intuitive, not much different than himself. His intuitive, American Indian side was a dating nightmare for my suitors and me. By the time I was able to date, at the raw age of 16, he would make sure the porch light mysteriously flickered until I was safely returned. I quickly learned how to agree with my father's expectations, and then go about doing what my adventurous side wanted to do. Less than truthful, it was a dreadful necessity early in life.

It wasn't until I became a mother that I appreciated my own mother's sensitive, softer side, often mistaken as weakness in my younger years. She had premonitions, visions, and encounters with angels twice during near-death experiences and always during the harder times of despair as a young woman. Often, these sensitivities worked to my advantage.

Once she had a mistaken vision of me as an unhappily married woman who fell victim to an unfortunate early death. That summer, before my junior year started, I was whisked off for a European vacation she believed might be our last big time together. We laughed and cried on that trip. We made up songs and sang. It was wonderful. Those carefree days we shared abroad deepened our relationship from mother/daughter to a lifelong friendship we both treasure and continue to benefit from, internally and externally. Now, we continue to enjoy our early bonding ritual, often over the telephone.

While the softer, feminine aspect of intuition was part of my life, it was purpose and determination that propelled me. In high school, I spent time helping children in hospitals and reading to the elderly. In college, I spent a year welcoming and teaching art to the returning veterans of Viet Nam. It was my first in-depth look at the effects of violence. I had never looked into the eyes of terror or shame before, and my heart wanted to help the brave young men who were coming of age through a loss of youth and joy.

Unfortunately, this focus on devastation, coupled with my natural healing abilities, led me to believe I could heal through immature love. As a result, I ended up in a violent marriage with two small, frightened children. After nine educational years, with only a quarter for a call, a baby on my arm, and a tiny little hand to hold, I left. Guilt and anger eventually led to compassion and forgiveness, but not without a price.

After my brave exit, I felt myself dying inside and out. Feelings of failure from my inability to protect my children from violence surfaced. Thoughts of love gave way to thoughts of anger and hatred. I was awash in negativity, and my body succumbed. I endured extreme migraine headaches and eventually had organ problems. There was little choice but to find my way back to that Secret Place of the Most High within.

Then, finally, one morning I awoke free, overwhelmed with a sense of lasting unconditional love and forgiveness for the father of my children. The power of that moment changed my life forever and gave me a profound understanding of the achievements we can embrace should we choose a life of compassion and love.

Firmly on my spiritual path once again, I was able to reignite my harmonious, intuitive side, calm my mind, and know the full joy of being a woman.

I busied myself creating a successful business empire, but my spirit ached for a partner for myself and a father figure for my children. I knew re-marrying would be a risk, but when I met a man with four children of his own, I fell in love with all of them. I spent the next 24 years raising and caring for our family – a task I considered my hardest and most important.

Many years later, after the children were grown and the marriage ultimately withered, I purchased an organic farm on Kauai, affectionately called "The Flower." There, I enjoyed the solitude of nature, and I met another man – this one very different than any I had known before.

We met at a Kahuna's wedding, at the far end of Kauai in a place the Dalai Lama fondly calls the "Eye of God." It is no ordinary place – you have to helicopter in, hike 11 miles of sheer cliff, or swim the deep ocean to grace its shores. The chance meeting carried intrigue: there, in Kalalau Valley, he extended his hand to help me safely cross the river.

It turned out we had much in common. We are both visionaries, we play tennis and enjoy swimming, and we both have cautious, independent natures. As years passed, we became further and further entwined. Then, in 2010, we decided to partner and create something we thought important in these changing times.

With his extensive connection to thinkers worldwide and my media experience as a TV producer/director, we created and survived the making of an astounding inspirational film: "Tapping the Source – One Voice, Many Faces." It was a crazy ride from start to finish. In just seven months, we filmed nearly 130 of the world's finest leaders and sacred sites, intuitively edited over 60 hours of footage, and packaged and marketed the finished film. I believe it was our continual closeness with The Secret Place of the Most High that enabled us to bring the project to fruition.

Looking back on my life thus far, I have been a conscientious daughter, a diligent wife and mother, and a support to my business partners. In each of these roles, I learned great lessons. But what stays with me now, as we enter what many believe to be a unique window of transformation for all humanity, is that ultimately it is my intuitive feminine nature – not the roles I have played – that teaches me best.

It is the intuitive nature of all women that will guide the coming century. Not the ability to outperform males in male-oriented roles or to perpetuate a society that is too often full of competition and short-term goals. Being a woman who follows her intuition carries a unique power. The power is breathtaking at times, but only one breath is needed to find faith in the next step. Staying in a state of love – whether with another, ourselves, or our divine purpose – gives hope to a weary world. When we acknowledge, accept, and allow our beauty as women to shine, then we will have done all that is needed to save the world.

It is my feminine nature that gives me strength when all seems lost. It is my feminine nature that encourages me to love when love is not encouraged. It is my feminine nature that allows me to take on the impossible and stay connected to the true miracle of life. It is The Secret Place of the Most High, my "inner voice," that connects me to all there is. Let us all rejoice in our deepest feminine knowledge. Let us – for the good of all humanity – stay vigilant about accessing and protecting this unlimited feminine awareness and power.

. . . .

Gayle Newhouse has produced and directed television shows and managed top artists such as Hoyt Axton. A talented film editor and set designer, Newhouse is co-producer and primary editor for "Tapping the Source." She is a trustee of the international think tank Club of Budapest, which includes founder Dr. Ervin Laszlo and honorary members Dr. Jane Goodall, the Dalai Lama, Mikhail Gorbachev, and Peter Gabriel.

Gayle has discovered a permanent way to change lives through the 24-week "Tapping the Source, the Original Course." This course is being offered to schools for young adults and to adults who want to commit to learning how to focus the mental mind, physical body, and emotional energies to position the subconscious mind for health, wealth, and love. www.tappingthesourcemovie.com

Let Your Heart Decide, Let Your Spirit Guide

By Amethyst Wyldfyre, multidimensional visionary, transformational spiritual leader, and host of the international radio show, "Blazing Forth the Light"

. . . .

I was traveling with one of my dearest friends through the heart of central Vermont, and along the way, on Route 100 near Granville Reservation, we saw a most magnificent waterfall. Melting snow poured from the heart of the mountain, out of an opening that was eerily reminiscent of a woman's body, and cascaded over massive rocks and stones framed by the evergreens and still dormant brown-grey branches of the deciduous trees. Simply standing in the presence of nature's brilliance and feeling the flow of life returning to the earth on this early spring day was perfect inspiration.

Up until 10 years ago, connections with the flow of nature were not even in my awareness. I was a typical "Type A" woman on a mission – highly regimented, my life structured down to the minute, no room for mistakes, better get it done and with a sense of urgency, if you please! My "masculine" side was out in full force, and I was marching in lockstep with the collective dream to work hard, find a mate, buy a house, have children, succeed at all costs, and acquire as many material goods as possible.

I was at the top of my game the year I turned 38. I had achieved all I had set out to achieve and then some. I had finished that year as the National Chairwoman of my trade association and had finalized the development, construction, and sale of an award-winning, multi-use residential and commercial real estate project. Inside, though, I was dying. When I realized my marriage wasn't working, I filed for divorce and began the (at first unconscious) journey to awaken the Divine Feminine within.

Our culture, up until recently, hasn't been known for its celebration of the gifts of the feminine. As a female, I was never encouraged to explore my intuition, my inherent healing capacities, or my creative side. The focus in my life was always super practical, primarily focused on making sure there was enough money to put bread on the table – a powerful masculine quality, to be sure, and an important one when you are the primary source of income in the household. But, it wasn't until I was liberated from my marriage that

I found myself in circumstances, like my first yoga classes, where I was encouraged to look at my heart, where I was openly asked to contemplate the question: "What is it that you want?"

I feel that feminine qualities – the feminine qualities that will save the world – originate in the heart. I say "feel," not "think," because thinking has been our default mode for too long. We must celebrate feeling over thinking if we mean to correct the imbalance that currently exists in the world. The capacity to marry the feminine with the masculine, to have both dance in balance with each other, to come into Divine Union – this is the objective of my own personal quest. And, ultimately, it is this delicate balance that also will bring peace and harmony to our planet. The masculine qualities of focus, concentration, alertness, action, and structure are necessary to counterbalance the feminine qualities of imagination, artistry, patience, receptivity, and wild abandon.

My own personal journey into my sacred feminine side revealed an abundance of hidden gifts, talents, and skills that I had never even imagined I possessed. As I asked power questions: "Who am I?" and "What do I want?" I activated and initiated a powerful process within myself.

Almost immediately after my divorce was final, it became clear that I needed to release my work, in addition to my marriage. After 18 years of building my career in common interest community management, consulting, and development, I knew I had to leave that work and the relationship with my male business partner behind.

One day in early December, I went in to the office and announced I was leaving. When my partner asked me what I was going to do to earn a living, I answered, "I'm going to be a crystal healer." I had no idea where those words came from; I'd never even *experienced* a crystal healing! But, it felt right. The path was set, and I made a leap into the great unknown.

The following years served as an inner world exploration that included enormous amounts of healing, reconciliation, and discovery for me. I spent the first two years mostly sitting in meditation on the floor of my living room, playing with crystals, making jewelry, exploring metaphysics, reading oracle cards, making art – and wondering what the heck I was doing living on MasterCard, Visa, American Express, Discover and the savings I had accumulated over my 18-year career when I had a small child to support and a roof to keep over our heads!

There was fear – plenty of it – and often the thought would pass through my mind that I must be crazy. This thought was echoed by the family and friends I was quickly outgrowing, who just didn't understand that I needed to take time to harmonize and heal – to explore and expand – to discover and delve into the depths of my being. You can't heal 20 years of imbalance in only a few minutes. Time is a necessary ingredient in the process – time to explore, time to engage in healing practices, time to integrate, time to decide where to explore next, time to be free to follow the whims and gentle urgings of the heart, time to come into the right relationship with the heart, time to bring the heart and mind together in harmony.

This was feminine work, this inner world exploration – the feminine at its finest. When we are able to harness that deep feminine capacity to delve into the dark – to go into the unknown to face fears, to bring a bright shining light of our awareness to the depths of our being for healing, illumination, and revelation – then we are able to release and let go of the pain, suffering, drama, trauma, and disharmonious energy we carry within. When we access the Divine Feminine capacity to hold pain; face the unknown and move through it with grace, openness, and the intention to be aware; and bring what is in us up and out – birth our blessings and our hidden gifts into the world – then and only then can the world around us change and grow into greater balance, more harmony, and infinitely more peace.

The battle of the sexes – the duality that is created when we separate, when we disconnect from the truth of what is – can only be healed by embracing both aspects of our beings: the hidden feminine and the exposed masculine. Learning to honor and acknowledge the fact that we are made of both of these energies is the greatest gift we can give to ourselves and to our planet.

Getting deeply in touch with my own heart was one of the greatest blessings of my inner journey. As a result, I cultivated a capacity to listen, to be still and allow myself to surrender to guidance from a force beyond my rational mind. The building of a relationship with my own heart meant cultivating time and space to sit with my heart, accessing the depths of my soul through my heart center, beginning the slow process of learning to trust again, and recovering from the betrayal of self that occurred when I had polarized into my masculine. This was a vital part of reclaiming my power.

Forgiveness was another piece of my re-balancing. To heal, we must find the way to forgiveness. We must learn to let go of the past, of guilt, blame, shame, anger, hatred, sadness, and remorse. We must surrender and free ourselves from the weight of carrying all these heavy energies. I feel that forgiveness is somehow connected to our ability as women to let go of our attachment to our creations (including our children.) Somewhere in the Feminine is the amazing capacity to create in full love and abandon – and then let the creation be free to find its own way in the world. The capacity to let go, again and again and again, and to use the freed-up energy to create anew puts us in divine order and aligns us with the natural rhythms and cycles of life and with the natural order of Mother Earth.

This creation process is an act of beauty. Finding and beginning to walk the beauty way, experiencing an overwhelming urge to create and the desire to bring beauty into the world, was the greatest gift of my own awakening. My world exploded open when I discovered and accessed the source of all creation, and let my heart decide and the spirit guide as to how that source would express itself through me.

To be in faith is to allow the Divine Masculine electrical energy to flow through us, to become conscious vessels through which this energy travels and is grounded in the Divine Feminine magnetic Earth. This is the secret to all manifestation (or Femifestation, if you prefer!) My prayer is to be clear – to be the pure, clear channel through which Spirit delivers inspiration – and, in full partnership with Earth, co-create expressions of these visions into physical form.

In my work with evolving entrepreneurs, we explore how the discovery of our passionate purpose must be channeled into the right relationship through entrepreneurialism. Our businesses become the vessel through which our gifts are delivered to the world in exchange for energy in the form of money. The dance of the right relationship between the masculine and feminine qualities shows up all the time in our interactions with our businesses. I find it deeply joyful to facilitate the beautiful bonding of the spiritual and the practical that allows for spiritually energized entrepreneurial success. I have found that this work is just another level of the dance reflected in my own inner world, in my relationship with my own business, in the work of my clients, and ultimately in our global evolutionary process.

As a fine philosopher once said, "As above, so below; as within, so without." When we finally honor the Feminine in each of us; when we acknowledge and take responsibility for the nurturing of our own hearts; when we admit to ourselves how we have abandoned, denigrated, sabotaged, and disregarded our own deep, intuitive, spiritual nature, we can then begin the process of rebuilding our inner relationship and coming into right relationship with all of life.

This is great work. It is the work that all of us – man and woman – must do in order to create the changes we dream of and desire in the core of our beings. The dream of a world where woman and man stand in partnership, where brothers and sisters around the globe recognize each other as all sharing the same breath, and where the children we birth are free to play, express, and be safe to explore all of who they are – human and Divine in harmony, peace and freedom from fear.

....

Amethyst Wyldfyre, the speaker's shaman and empowered messenger master mentor, is a multidimensional visionary healer, speaker, performer, author, teacher, and artist passionate about serving visionary leaders and conscious entrepreneurs who want to LEAP fearlessly into their highest level of service to the planet – and who want to profit handsomely from following their spiritual path.

She is in service to the empowerment of global messengers of change and invested in supporting big visionaries find their authentic voice, crystallize their message, stand strong in speaking their truth, and cultivate a commanding, magnetic presence so they feel safe, powerful, and prepared to be heard by millions. Amethyst is an initiated Shamaness in the Inka tradition, a naturally-ordained Crystal Singing Bowl Sound Therapist, and an author of several books. She has appeared on Amazon and Barnes & Noble bestselling lists, is featured on radio and TV, and was selected in 2008 by NH Magazine as a Renaissance Woman. She is a multiple award winning entrepreneur, juried artist, and, in 2009, her "Divine Union - A Crystal Singing Bowl Healing Journey" CD was a COVR AWARD Winning Finalist at the International New Age Trade Show in Denver. Visit www.theempoweredmessenger.com.

I am Intuitive.

1. I acknowledge that I know what is best for me.

2. I acknowledge that all others know what is best for them.

3. I allow myself quiet time so my inner voice becomes clearer.

4. I notice physical symptoms and environmental cues, in order to clarify any intuitive messages I may not understand.

5. I recognize that I have access to the collective unconscious of all women of all times, and I use this knowledge to assist me.

nurturing

Mother Teresa

"The woman is the heart of the home. Let us pray that we women realize the reason of our existence: to love and be loved and through this love become instruments of peace in the world." – Mother Teresa

Mother Teresa of Calcutta, also known as the Angel of Mercy and the Saint of the Gutter, is an iconic figure famous for her compassionate and nurturing nature, which she demonstrated through her lifelong service to the poor.

Born of Albanian descent on August 26, 1910, in what is now Skopje, Macedonia, Agnes Gonxha Bojaxhiu received her calling to God at age 12. Six years later, at 18, she left home to pursue a lifetime of service to God. She was given the name Sister Teresa and began her service with the Sisters of Loreto, first as a teacher and later as a principal at a school for girls in Calcutta, India. On May 24, 1937, she took her Final Procession of Vows and became known as Mother Teresa.

In 1946, she received inspiration from Jesus to devote her life to the poorest of the poor by living among them. From this, she founded the Missionaries of Charity in 1950 and began her work in the slums of India. Immensely humble, Mother Teresa became known for her intimate care of others – she cleaned wounds, fed the starving, and prayed with the despondent. Her work, however, also brought her a sense of personal torment; she felt an intense separation from God and an immersion in the painful belief that she was united with Jesus in her thirst for love.

Eventually, around 4,000 of her Charity Sisters performed similar acts of kindness in 123 countries around the world. A million co-workers worked in more than 600 missions, which included hospices; homes for those with HIV/AIDS, leprosy, and tuberculosis; orphanages; counseling programs; soup kitchens; and schools. When Mother Teresa died in Calcutta in 1997, the Church moved quickly to canonize her as a saint. On October 19, 2003, Pope John Paul II beatified her in St. Peter's Square before a crowd of several hundred thousand people. Her feast day within the Catholic faith is September 5. The day she died is considered a public holiday in Albania, and is referred to as "Mother Teresa Day."

. . . .

• Awarded the Pope John XXIII Peace Prize in 1971

• Won the Nobel Peace Prize in 1979

• Received India's highest civilian award, the Bharat Ratna, in 1980

• Received the Legion d'Honneur from Jean-Claude Duvalier in 1981

• Brokered a temporary cease-fire between the Israeli Army and Palestinian guerillas during the Siege of Beirut, in 1982

• Traveled through a war zone with Red Cross workers to rescue dozens of hospitalized children, some of whom were handicapped

• Received a U.S. Medal of Freedom in 1985, a Congressional Gold Medal in 1994, and honorary U.S. citizenship in 1996

• Continued her work even after heart attacks, the insertion of a pacemaker, and pneumonia

Florence Nightingale

"I think one's feelings waste themselves in words; they ought all to be distilled into actions, which bring results." – Florence Nightingale

Florence Nightingale embraced a calling to care for the sick. She improved worldwide standards in the nursing profession and in medical care and ultimately saved millions of lives.

....

Florence Nightingale was born on May 12, 1820, in Florence, Italy to wealthy landowner William Nightingale. He took personal responsibility for Florence's education and taught her languages, the sciences, history, philosophy, and mathematics. As Florence grew older, she felt stifled by the traditional limitations placed on women's activities, and spent a great deal of her time at hospitals in England, where she became fond of caring for the poor and the sick.

At age 17, she felt called by God toward a great cause. Over the years, she rejected many suitors, and, at 25, she informed her parents she wanted to be a nurse, a profession considered beneath her social stature.

Four years later, Florence traveled to Egypt, where she met the nuns of St. Vincent de Paul in Alexandria, who impressed her with their disciplined methods for caring for the sick. A short while later, she met Elizabeth Blackwell, the first female doctor recognized by the United States. Further inspired to pursue her dreams of becoming a nurse, Florence finally obtained her father's permission in 1851 to begin training. She spent four months at the Institute of Protestant Deaconesses in Kaiserwerth, a training school for female teachers and nurses, and received her first position as the superintendent of the Institute for the Care of Sick Gentlewomen in 1853.

That same year, more than 8,000 British troops were struck by cholera and malaria in Turkey. It was the Crimean War, and there was a shortage of male doctors. Florence gained permission to travel to the region with 38 nurses to care for the wounded and sick. Once there, Florence realized the conditions of the warfront hospital were deplorable. Men were dying from infections and poor care. At first rebuffed for her assessment, Florence later publicized her criticisms of the hospital's conditions. The resulting public outcry allowed her to overtake and reconstruct the hospital's policies. Her reforms made a dramatic difference in the number of unnecessary deaths.

In addition to her work in Turkey, Florence founded a nursing school; acted as a medical consultant during both the American Civil War and the Franco-Prussian War; and helped establish the East London Nursing Society, the Workhouse Nursing Association, the National Society for Providing Trained Nurses for the Poor, and the Queen's Jubilee Nursing Institute. In 1857, she helped the Indian government establish a Sanitary Department. She also used her work to publish a popular book, "Notes on Nursing."

Florence died in London in 1910 at 90 years old. Memorial services took place in St. Paul's Cathedral and the Liverpool Cathedral, but many more services were held across the world.

. . . .

- One of the first recognized, professional nurses who earned due credit for the profession
- Brought the death rate to 2% in military hospitals during the Crimean War
- Awarded Royal Red Cross by Queen Victoria 1883
- Was the first woman awarded the Order of Merit, which she received in 1907
- Awarded the Freedom of the City of London in 1908
- Awarded the German order of the Cross of Merit
- Awarded the French gold medal of Secours aux Blessés Militaires
- Awarded the badge of honor of the Norwegian Red Cross Society in 1910

 **Essays By Women**

The Love That Carries Us Through

Dedicated to my mother, Joan Frances O'Keefe 1936-1996

By Kathleen Aston, speaker, author, mentor at Kathleen Aston International, LLC, and founder of International Association of Purpose-Driven Entrepreneurs

....

Ten years ago, I sat at the desk in my home office, my head down on folded arms, tears spilling onto the papers below. Each time I blinked, I saw the deluge of salty droplets mix with ink and run in tiny streams across the printed, paper sheets crumpled beneath my arms. I was coming to the end of it … to the end of two and a half years of entrepreneurship. Thirty months working 18-hour days, and collapsing at midnight into the rumple of blankets, sheets, and pillows strewn across my bed.

Even in sleep I could not escape the fear and worry that plagued me. Dreams of disaster flashed from my unconscious to my conscious and left my slumber broken in fits and starts. Every moment of my existence was consumed with the challenge of preventing my business – and my life – from careening out of control. On that fateful day ten years ago, I was certain each was jettisoning down its own icy runway to unavoidable emotional and financial bankruptcy.

In times like that one, and there had been countless in the preceding years, I could feel my mother's presence surround me. I could smell her perfume, hear her voice – that old, raspy record in my head set to play, skip, and repeat. "You come from strong stock," she'd say. "Pull yourself up by your bootstraps, and get going."

My mother was never one to tolerate self-pity or complaining. "I'll give you something to complain about …" was always her retort to whines that regaled life's imperfections and injustices. That day, her presence was strong. It always presented with an energy equal to or stronger than necessary to combat and subdue whatever pain prevailed in me at the time.

I sniffed, raised my head, wiped my eyes, and put my glasses back on – their bridge down toward the tip of my nose. I wore those glasses so many hours a day that the indent ridge between my eyes had become frighteningly permanent. I was experimenting with other places on which they could rest.

I sat back and lifted the financial printouts from the top of the paper pile. As I wiped off the tear-soaked page, I smeared some of the numbers. It didn't really matter at that point; I knew the bottom line.

I was $365,000 in debt.

My husband had Stage 4 Lymphoma. My son was mentally ill and recently had been diagnosed with severe bi-polar disorder, psychotic tendencies, and borderline schizophrenia. He was in a high-security school for mentally ill boys. My mother was dead. My younger daughter now resided with her father – because I had no way to keep her safe from her brother when he was still at home.

My life, my business, my dreams, and my hopes swirled in bloody tatters around me and rendered me fall-down dizzy. My mind teetered trying to comprehend the total devastation ... a total flattening of the city I had once proudly called My Life. A life dedicated to others, a life giving 100%, a life that sacrificed my own desires and well-being to serve others. I felt the fury start to bubble in the deep recesses of my soul. So, this is my reward, I thought bitterly. This is how it will all end ... how my efforts will be remembered.

In that moment, I bemoaned the hard work. I seethed with resentment of every hour wasted trying to do the right thing, the right way, with the right heart. I believed, in my dark despair, that I had been mocked by the universe and deceived by God. I looked up at my calendar and noted the date that would, from here on out, mark the death of my hopes and dreams.

On that day, I would have no choice but to let go of it all – the dreams, elations, tears, exhaustion, victories, terrors. All of it was going up in a silent but deadly mushroom cloud. At that moment, losing everything was just a heartbeat away. Losing my mind was closer.

"Stop wallowing." My mother's whisper was so real I could almost feel her warm, moist breath in my ear.

I could feel the tears begin again. They welled up and tumbled quietly down my cheeks as I looked at the financial spreadsheets one last time, as if by will I might make the numbers dance, switch partners, and transpose from negative into positive.

"Oh, my God! Why did I do all this?" I sobbed.

"For love." Her whisper was stronger, closer. "You did it all for love, Kathleen."

I sat back, wiped my eyes once more, and took deep breaths to relieve the tension in my chest. My teeth chattered, even though the room was warm. My nerves had gotten the better of me.

So all this pain comes down to love? That couldn't be right. In fact, that was insane. I stopped to think. Was it love that had gotten me here? That question hung in the air around me. Although I hadn't spoken it aloud, it permeated every oxygen cell in the room, lingered in every corner. The answer came as a resounding, "Yes."

At such a moment, I imagine many would swear off doing anything for love again. But, my mother had reared me well. I was programmed, wired, to accept that acts of true love, even if they ended disastrously, were only good and could never be bad. I had been faithful and enduring. I had fought until the seemingly looming end.

"Don't give up." This time it was the whisper of my own voice I heard. "Don't give up."

I began to frame my decisions in a new light. I had started my business to create more earnings so that I could care for my mentally ill son and my ailing husband, so I could create a way to continually take care of them as the worst continued to unfold. I had moved my daughter to live with her father and grandparents to save her from physical harm. That was love, to give her up, to keep her safe and well from a brother who threatened her life. I had bought this big house, far away from the little home I had loved so much, to combine my business and home so that when my husband's remission ended, I could work at home to care and be near him.

It was true. I had done everything for love. A fierce desire to protect those I loved. And, that blind passion fueled a powerful determination to provide and ensure survival for all under my care.

"Survive. Don't give up." I repeated. And, I picked up the phone and dialed.

My colleague and friend arrived later that morning. I handed him the sob-soaked financial spreadsheets, and he sat down with me and started to teach me the business of *doing* business.

And the miracle? In eighteen months, I went from being $365,000 in debt to billing over $1.8 million dollars. Today, I know with certainty that it was the relentless power of my feminine attribute to love and nurture, mixed with the pinnacle attributes of my feminine power to seek to understand, collaborate, and, above all else, ensure the survival of my family – that turned the tide.

At the Vancouver Peace Summit in September 2009, the Dalai Lama stated that the world would be saved by the Western woman. I have ruminated on this deeply, and I agree. Western women have had to merge their feminine energy, which radiates nurturance, collaboration, compassion, and empathy, with a masculine energy to accomplish, protect, and get results.

Western women, in their fight for rights and equality, have had to learn to play in "a man's world" by learning how to be a bit more masculine than women in other countries. As such, we now are becoming the major force in business and job creation. Businesses are seeking out ways to incorporate more feminine approaches to create healthier, happier, more prosperous work environments. Survival – on a national and global basis – is starting to rest on the Western woman's ability to use her innate feminine energy with her assumed masculine energy to be more powerful and influential than ever before.

Through my ability to seek help in the dark despair, through my willingness to admit certain defeat, through my desire for collaboration, I harnessed the pinnacle attributes of my feminine power. And, I turned the tides of destruction into peaceful waves of prosperity and security. I did not become hateful or bitter, although I had moments of such emotions. I never lost my humanity, my passion, or my will to survive.

Women are not just valuable to humanity, they are essential. For what is a world without a great Mother? What is a world void of nurturance, compassion, empathy, and collaboration? It is a heartless world – cold and without understanding. Nurturing is the essential ingredient; nurturing must take place if an inkling of greater understanding is to exist at all. If a world is without compassion for ones' self or others, it is a world filled with hopeless souls who have nothing to lose except the mere agony of life itself. We are blessed with the task of honoring the life birthed in the womb of women, as well as the passionate feminine love that carries it through.

. . . .

Kathleen Aston is recognized as a leader in business, a million-dollar serial entrepreneur, and a women's empowerment leadership expert. With an experimental mindset and deep desire to create her own life of purpose-driven prosperity, she has dedicated her life to learning and leveraging the habits and behaviors implemented by the world's most successful business icons.

By leveraging her own life-journey of transformation in conjunction with her coaching, leadership, and productivity certifications, Kathleen is active in women's centers for enterprise, entrepreneurship, and professional and spiritual development. She is revered for her ground-breaking perspectives and approaches that transform the lives of women nationwide. Kathleen is a "force" on stage as an incomparable speaker, facilitator, and mentor. She carries her profound message of courage, confidence, and prosperity to women seeking game-changing "inside-out" transformations in their businesses and lives. She is the founder of Kathleen Aston International (Boston Area) and the author of "Precious Pain and Promises," as well as the recent founder of the International Association of Purpose-Driven Entrepreneurs. www.kathleenastonintl.com

Ageless Beauty, Eternal Feminine

By Shirley W. Mitchell, author of "Sensational after 60®: Loving Life All Over Again" and owner-celebrity talk show host of the Aging Outside the Box® syndicated media group

. . . .

There is a certain magic about women, and for me, becoming a mother is a large part of embracing this feminine splendor. I grew up in the South and was raised on a cotton farm with my brother and sister in a traditional Christian family. There was no divorce in my immediate family tree, and my siblings and I were lucky to live close to both sets of our grandparents.

My parents, brother and sister, grandparents, uncles, aunts, and cousins worked the white fields of cotton as a team. We attended church, socialized, and prayed together. We lived off the products of our land. We grew our vegetables, milked our cows, churned our butter, and gathered eggs from our chickens. Our meat was produced on our 60-acre farm.

Sunday, after church service, our family and the ministers gathered at my grandmother's table, which was always loaded with delicious food. While the adults gathered in the afternoon to discuss politics, world affairs, and faith, the children played games such as "Knock the Tin Can" and "Red Rover, Red Rover." In the middle of the afternoon, a huge tub of homemade ice cream was cranked by hand in a wooden freezer. The crowning event of every Sunday was fellowship over ice cream. As I observed my grandmother, mother, and aunts coordinate the weekly festivities, I learned that strong Christian women were the heart of the home. Their nurturance was the thread that sewed the family together.

Naturally, I grew to believe that becoming a mother was my high calling. At 21, I married the man I loved. Together, we raised three precious children, all of whom were cherished by a loving, extended family. I feel blessed that God entrusted me with children, and all three have grown into family-oriented, Christian business people in their own rights. They have delighted me with ten grandchildren and two great-grandchildren – my reassurance that chariots of angels surround us as we travel this precious road of life.

I view my grandchildren as a caress from God. Just as I began to miss having my own children so present in my life, He gifted me with grandchildren. To nurture their spirits, and my own, I began a tradition of taking my grandchildren on a personal vacation to a destination of their choice when they turn ten. I love traveling with ten year olds! They have stars and wonderment in their eyes as they visit new places and learn new things. Their exuberance is spirit-lifting.

My oldest granddaughter, Michelle, chose Washington, D.C., for her trip. She is a beauty, and at age ten, she looked 15. The first morning we were in Washington, D.C., we boarded a tram to the White House. A sign stated, "Children and Seniors Free." When Michelle got on the tram, the operator did not believe she was ten because she looked like a teen, and she had to pay full price. With my stilettos and fashion sense, the operator would not believe I was a senior citizen. I gladly paid the full fare! What fun we had laughing about our plight.

Though I loved my years of youth – dancing to Elvis Presley music and experiencing the magic of new romance and blossoming sexuality – I recently have awakened to what I call "ageless living." Ageless living is an awareness that under the wrinkles and gray hair, there's still a young girl inside. To nourish her and nurture her, I've learned to follow my passions of writing, speaking, and becoming a radio talk show host. After a painful divorce I didn't want, I've also found that romance in older life is of an even greater intensity than romance in youth!

When Michelle graduated high school, I drove from Alabama to Cincinnati, Ohio, for her graduation and party. Not yet having awakened to my ageless living, I felt I needed to present a well-groomed, youthful appearance to the world. Since I am allergic to the sun, I decided to get a spray tan the day before my drive.

The young spa employee's eye makeup and plump red lips were immaculate, and I complimented her appearance. She informed me she had the ability to give me permanent eye make-up and lip color. At 65, my lips were fading in color, and my eyelashes were thin so I agreed. I did not even think to consider that the procedure was a tattoo. But, after a few minutes with the needle, I realized it was definitely a tattoo!

But, this is good, I thought. I'll look younger!

As I paid my bill, the tattoo artist said, "I hope you are not going to be in public for a few days, to give time for the swelling to go down." My heart sank. I told her I was supposed to drive to Cincinnati the next day for my oldest granddaughter's high school graduation and party for her friends and family. She looked regretful and said, "Try putting Vaseline on your lips tonight. Maybe that will help!"

During the night, my lips begin to swell ... and swell. I got out of bed, and in the dim light of the bathroom, accidently applied "Preparation H" to my lips instead of Vaseline!

The next morning, my lips looked like big, red balloons, and there was no way to hide them. But, I spoke firmly to myself: "I will not allow pride to keep me from my granddaughter's graduation!" I wore sunglasses to cover my eyes, and I made the drive.

And, I am so glad I did. I was blessed to witness my granddaughter sing a solo in the program, and I am so thankful I was present to share in that moment. Of course, not wanting to press my luck, I stayed out of the family photos! At many family gatherings since that day, this story has been a big part of our entertainment. It's a fun story to share – now. It's fun to laugh, even when it's at our own expense, and I think this is part of the brilliance of understanding this sense of ageless beauty. The inner beauty, the inner light and joy, are eternal.

During the 1980s, my children's father and I were honored along with a half dozen other grocery professional couples to be hosted by the Russian government. Our mission was to help them bring their grocery standards up to levels comparable to the United States. To put it mildly, the trip behind the Iron Curtain gave me great reason to appreciate the supermarket where I shopped in America. Groceries in Moscow were sold from a variety of vendors. Dairy products were in one shop, displayed in small cases in clear, plastic bags with no labels. Down the street would be a small meat market, where meat hung from the ceiling with no wrapping. Long lines of people waited to buy from vendors in the street, selling heads of cabbage out of a wheelbarrow.

We were told that many women spent the entire day searching for food for dinner for their households. I could see the panic on their faces as they scurried from shop to shop. It felt like almost all the Russian women were overworked and tired. And, to me, they looked sad. I came away from the trip with a great respect for the Russian women who labored, shopped, and fed their families from the cramped, dirty specialty shops. I stood in admiration of their fortitude.

During the Cold War with the United States, Russian women were not what we may think of as "feminine," but they were stout and they were strong. The trip helped me realize that this, too – this ability to be strong in the face of adversity, to feed and nourish and take care of our families to the best of our abilities no matter the circumstances – transcends geographical lines and is a large part of our nature as women. I honor and celebrate all strong women all over the world who are experiencing hard lives and difficulty in feeding their families. Fierce like a mother bear, the female spirit protects her cubs from harm and nurtures them toward growth.

In this millennium, it seems women will be a driving force in business, education, military, entertainment, and political arenas – while also being the heart of the home and the heart of the world. Today, women are breaking away from traditional business models and creating new, collaborative ones that encourage consensus and positive outcomes for all. Through our ability to collaborate and be supportive of each other, we are constructing feminine models that will nurture and serve the world in new and unexpected ways. My own business and entrepreneurial spirit, writing and selling books, speaking to 161 countries as a radio talk show host, and traveling to speaking engagements, feeds my soul. I believe my own example is indicative of countless women experiencing this same kind of exhilaration from self-creation and self-nurturance.

One of my favorite role models is beloved actress, entrepreneur, and billionaire Elizabeth Taylor. She was the epitome of a multicolored female spirit and ageless beauty! She exemplified royalty with her splendor and grace, and she remained gracious and classy through tragedy and triumph. She dedicated herself to humanitarian causes, lit a spark to wipe out AIDS, and she always believed in love. Like many other women around the world, through her passion and dedication, she made the world a better place.

As females, we create this miracle of life in birth, and we also help create the miraculous lives that develop from it. We are strong, we are tender, and our spirit is one of ageless beauty. And, this is how we rock the cradle of the world.

....

Shirley W. Mitchell is the owner-celebrity talk show host of the Aging Outside the Box® syndicated media group, which includes Aging Outside the Box® and Aging Outside the Box® Christian Spiritual Sparks™. Known as "The Golden Egg of Aging™," Shirley is the author of ten books, including "Fabulous after 50® Finding Fulfillment for Tomorrow," and "Sensational after 60® Loving Life All Over Again." She also is co-author of five books, including: "101 Great Ways to Improve Your Life." She is a columnist of the syndicated "Fabulous after Fifty™" online column and a featured columnist for Senior Lifestyle Magazine.

As an aging and longevity expert, Shirley is recognized as one of the top writers and speakers on aging, seniors, the Baby Boomer Generation, women's issues, and healthy lifestyles. She is a member of American Society on Aging, American Senior Benefits Association, National Association for Female Executives, International Women's Leadership Association, American Business Women's Association, Red Hat Society, Diva Web of Fame, and The Lit Chicks of Sand Mountain. Managed and represented by Lighthouse Coastal Productions, her online enterprise comprises 59 websites, 13 blogs, and two dozen social sites, including Self Growth, Inc. She supports the American Heart Association and the Go Red for Women Program. www.agingoutsidethebox.net

Mother's Milk

By Lorelei Shellist, spiritual psychologist, author, speaker, minister, and life coach

....

The root of the word "nurture" is Latin and means both "to nourish" and "to feed." My own definition of nurturing is feeding, and the most nourishing fluid we can feed a baby is milk: mother's milk. Being held as a baby and being breastfed is soothing and nourishing – the epitome of nurturance.

I was bottle-fed. As I reflect on my life, I think I was always looking for the breast, the breast of love, that missing link to love. I think I must have felt that disconnect when I first was put on the bottle, and this disconnected me from my mother in a subtle but profound way. Not that my mother was to blame. It was the 1960s, and being able to feed your baby from a bottle was new and convenient, especially if you were a working mother, which my mother was.

Looking back, I realize I was always searching for nurturance. One of my favorite lyrics comes from a song performed by Grace Jones, "from the nipple to the bottle, never satisfied." This speaks volumes, especially for people with addictions to alcohol, cigarettes, and food. We try to self-medicate, to "nurse" ourselves. Oral addiction, the drive to find something to put in our mouths that will soothe us, is a search for loving nurturance.

I learned to nurture myself early in life, too early for a child. Luckily, I was born independent. As a little girl, I practiced nurturance on my dolls. My favorite doll was Chatty Kathy, who had a string I could pull to make her talk. Chatty Kathy could say, "I love you" and "Please take me with you," among other things. She nurtured me with her kind words as I nurtured her with care and love, until my heart reached out for another doll: "Little Miss No Name."

Little Miss No Name was an orphan doll who wore a brown burlap sack for a dress. She had big, brown, cow-pie eyes and a teardrop that ran down her cheek. I yearned to adopt her because I thought she needed me, or at least my nurturance. She needed a mother's love, a mother who would take care of her. From the age of six, my entelechy was in place: I would rescue, mother, serve, and nurture those who needed me most.

It's no wonder that, by the time I was 23, I was well practiced in nurturing others and had fallen in love with an alcoholic. I had learned to put others' needs before my own until my well ran dry. I was just reaching my thirties when I consciously discovered my pattern of mothering others, and I was well into my forties before I could even begin to break out of the habit. It took the death of my fiancé, Steve Clark, to bring me to my knees.

Steve was one of the most gifted songwriters and guitarists in the world. His successes with the rock band Def Leppard were numerous, and he lived what most people would define as a very charmed life. But, Steve had a serious drinking problem he relied on to fill the void and give him what he called "Dutch courage."

I spent years trying to help him, take care of him, lead him to the well … but I couldn't make him drink from the nurturing waters of "self-love" no matter how hard I tried. He used the bottle to nurture himself, and all the nurturance I could muster could not save him. So at thirty years old, a glowing young man with the world at his fingertips, Steve dimmed his own light and quietly slipped away.

I wrote in my first book, "Runway RunAway," that it was in losing Steve that I found myself. And, once I found myself, there was no turning my back on *me* ever again. After Steve's death, I had to learn to take care of myself, instead of others – and there was a lot to learn.

The professors Dr. Ron and Mary Hulnick at the University of Santa Monica remind students all the time: "Take care of your self so you can then take care of others." Everyone talks about "loving yourself." They say, "You have to love yourself first." But, how do we do that? Where do we begin? I say, "Start with nurturing your self!"

Feed your self first, so you can then feed others with love, care, compassion, and grace. Anyone who has ever flown on an airplane has heard the flight attendants' instructions to "place the oxygen mask on yourself first" in the event of an emergency. We all know what would happen if we tried to put the mask on another first ... we would suffocate and die in the process. Yet, that is exactly what many of us do all through our lives, and then we wonder why we are exhausted!

The answer is simple: we must take time to nurture ourselves.

Nurturing as a way of *being* is a feminine quality, but *doing* something nurturing is a masculine quality. The balance of these qualities lies at the heart of the Authentic Self – our spirit, our essence, which has no gender. But, how can we be and do at the same time? Learning how to nurture ourselves offers us a graceful opportunity to find this balance and answer this question.

The AA 12-Step program uses an anagram called HALT. It is what the program encourages when you find yourself short fused, acting out, or triggered. You ask, what do I need right now? Am I **H**ungry? Am I **A**ngry? Am I **L**onely? Am I **T**ired? Chances are if we tend to these basic needs and nourish ourselves with tender loving care, we will feel better right away. We will be at peace again.

When we ask a question to our higher selves, listen to the answer, and take our own advice, a shift immediately takes place within our consciousness. Right away, our spirit, our inner child, feels taken care of, seen, and heard. Our self feels fed, loved, and nurtured.

Self-nurturing is a way of giving to, and receiving from ourselves. It is a process of remembering ourselves, putting our selves back together with self-acceptance and self-care. It is a manner of returning home. So how do we do this? Where do we begin? I can't tell you how to do your own self-nurturing regime, but I can tell you how I do mine.

I start the day by checking in first with my self. As I awaken into my consciousness, I lie in bed and stretch my body from my head to my toes. I reconnect from my unconscious "dream state" into my awareness of the new day. I then hold still in my comfy bed as I try to remember my dreams. I stay with my self for as long as I want to stay; this is my quality time with me, and I smile in gratitude for another day.

If I wake up with any anxiety or negativity, I try to reframe those thoughts and return to gratitude again. If I can remember any dreams or fragments, I jot them down on paper that I keep by my bed. Then, I ask myself what I need next. Usually it's coffee! While it may not be the healthiest choice, coffee has become part of my ritual, the beginning of a ceremony that starts my day. All my days begin with this sacred ceremony through which I connect with God, the Higher Powers, the Buddha, the Christ, the Angels, and all the Ascended Masters and teachers that have ever been. I take time for this.

Time these days seems more precious than money, and so it is the most valuable thing I can offer to God and to myself. Time to pray, time to meditate, time to be with me. This is how I nurture myself on a spiritual level.

With coffee in hand, I sit in my sacred place, the altar I have created that holds all the little things I connect with – candles, photos, shells, effigies, crystals, angel cards, and other delightful treasures. There, I light a candle, and I begin to pray.

Sometimes I get emotional. I may tear up in sorrow for something I am losing or that I have lost. When that happens, I simply allow myself the time to grieve, without judgment. I let my tears be. When they are finished, I return to gratitude. Other times, I may tear up in joy. These are the moments when everything seems to be "ok" on the physical plane, and I rest in the knowledge and faith that "all is good." I trust then that I am provided for, and I allow myself my tears of joy.

I offer them, mixed with laughter, love, and grace, up to Spirit. I allow myself to feel my feelings. When I am angry or worried, I do a prayer of clearing. I track my thoughts and forgive myself for any misunderstandings I may be holding inside. I may write my negative feelings down and burn them ... thereby returning them to a far-off place where they may be of better use. This is how I nurture myself on an emotional level.

All through the day, I track my thinking, my eating, my chores, my choices. I try to stay true to the things I promise myself. I make a conscious decision to choose activities that are loving to me. When I get pulled in another direction, or tempted by distraction or unhealthy things, I ask myself, "Is this good for me? Is this a loving choice?"

Speaking my truth, honoring myself by listening to what I say I need or want, and then making self-honoring choices in order to have or be those things – these are gentle ways of setting boundaries. Boundaries feel masculine, where self-honoring choices feels feminine. So I also feed myself with nourishing books, documentaries, music, hobbies, foods, baths, creams, prayers, and other self-loving choices.

As I look at life in my rearview mirror, I see that though the visions appear to be smaller, I will never forget the impact my experiences have had on me. I realize that those mishaps, those heartbreaks, those losses, and those bottle-fed milk drops of life were all there to teach me how to give love to myself and to receive love from others. Nurturing myself on all levels – mind, body, heart, and soul – is how I remember myself to my self. It is a way to be with me.

The divine feminine nature that is inherent in all of us needs to help, take care of, and nurture others. These are our gifts to the world. But, we always must remember to gift ourselves with the loving, motherly milk of self-nurturance first.

. . . .

Author, Speaker, and Coach **Lorelei Shellist** brings new meaning to the term "supermodel." Lorelei writes candidly and boldly about life as a runway model and her struggles with her fiancé's addiction in "Runway RunAway: A Backstage Pass to Fashion, Romance & Rock 'N Roll." Her wit, sense of humor, and "perfect fit" measurements enabled her to serve as a muse for Karl Lagerfeld, YSL, La Croix, Bob Mackie, Geoffrey Beene, and Armani. Lorelei is featured internationally on TV, film, and radio: GMA, Inside Edition, AM NY, Phil Donahue, KTLA, CNN, BBC, Joan Rivers, and in the VH-1 Def Leppard "Behind the Music" documentary. Model Amber Valetta plays Lorelei in the VH-1 movie, "Hysteria" (Paramount.)

Life experiences have enabled Lorelei to inspire others with her story of survival and success. She counsels women in prison and at-risk teens, teaching critical "Life Skills." As an expert on beauty and women's issues, she encourages others to attract appropriate attention through conscious dressing, while having fun expressing themselves. A graduate of two Master's Programs: Spiritual Psychology and Consciousness Health & Healing at the University of Santa Monica, Lorelei's appeal crosses many demographics. Her ultimate goal is to help others manifest grace, joy, and authenticity in their lives. www.LoreleiShellist.com

Dreaming the Garden Goddess

By Dr. June Stinchfield, depth psychologist

....

An image of my hands in the earth keeps repeating itself in my mind's eye; it insists upon my attention. It's strange, but I can actually feel my hands reaching into the rich, dark soil. The cool dampness of it restores me. It has been some time since I have had the opportunity to tend a garden, and so I hearken to this simple image as a call to turn my attention to the soil, the plants, the flowers, the weeds, the bees, and the insects.

I am being called, but as I know from experience, the path is not always clear. Hands in the earth might mean many things. As a depth psychologist, I am always acutely aware of that which is hidden and the myriad ways in which the hidden calls to us to be discovered. I decide to allow the imagination to be my guide in traversing this particular path.

Our culture is dependent on left-brain modes of perception – the rational, unemotional, linear way of answering any question that presents itself. Since we were children, most of us have been taught that imagination is not a valid way of knowing. And yet, dreams, intuitions, and creative musings have been enormously helpful to me in my life, as they have been to my friends and patients.

I have found through my own experiences that the imagination is a way to make contact with the hidden, the often marginalized, and the ignored. The imagination, then, is a way to honor the feminine, receptive, creative, and sometimes chaotic aspects of our very beings and the part of myself, perhaps, that wants her hands in the earth.

It occurs to me that my interest in the garden and in tending the earth need not be as pretty and refined as first intended. The earth can represent something basic and instinctual. Its cycles and seasons reflect our own fertility, our own cycles. We, too, are caught in the rhythms of life, between birth and death. We, too, are constantly losing aspects of ourselves, and then undergoing renewal. Perhaps this is a time of new life for me, too.

I feel a need for community and connection to the place I now live. I need to nurture, to heal, to restore. In my neighborhood, I find a once lovely, but now neglected, garden. Its neglect reminds me of the feminine aspects of ourselves, the intuitive, dreamy parts, that we so often ignore. These areas are left untended while other areas are well cared for and loved. By joining the garden guild and helping to restore the garden, I will be honoring and restoring my feminine nature, as well as fostering the feminine values of community and connection. Here, with my hands in the earth, I can return a beloved resource to the community, one that can be enjoyed by all. Others, as well as myself, will be able to visit and find peace and solace in Nature's lovely arms.

It turns out, though, that some very determined daemon seems bent on keeping me from this work. It rains all spring in New York, and it is not a fine, misty rain, but a hard, driving one that keeps most gardeners indoors. Many phone calls to the museum garden are met with the admonition to stay away – it is too wet. I am anxious to get started, but the first volunteer day is not called until May. That morning, I gather my straw hat and my gardening gloves and drive to the garden, expecting to see a horde of volunteers.

I couldn't have been more wrong – and yet my thesis of the neglect of the feminine couldn't have been proven more right. Greeted by a group of only three stalwarts, I am instructed to take a wheelbarrow and spread mulch around the shrubs and trees. This is not at all what I'd envisioned, but I am open to anything and so dig in. It is laborious work, not at all like the romantic fantasy I'd had of gardening among the flowers. I do not get much contact with the other gardeners, and I can't help but notice as I work how sad the garden looks. There are too few gardeners to make a dent in the years of neglect. Everyone seems too discouraged to engage each other in conversation, and I begin to realize that my notion of being in Nature with kindred souls is not the way this experience is going to manifest. By the end of the day, my arms and legs ache. I have not been able to get my hands in the dirt, but I did spread some with a shovel, and I got to be outside on a beautiful, cool, spring day.

I continue to go to the garden, but most of these times I am alone. I don't feel a part of a community. There is a feeling of being stuck here, of things not growing, of almost being petrified in time. The work in this garden is one of maintenance. There is no sense of the continuation of life; there is no planting of new living beings or even a sense of tending to what few shrubs and trees do grow here. Like my fellow gardeners, I am discouraged, and I begin to feel as though I am not fulfilling psyche's task.

There has been too much solitude in my life ... too much stuck-ness ... and I find myself craving the company of others. I seek the liveliness of conversation and the connectedness of a community in which plants and humans are each a part of the glorious whole. I see myself reflected in this garden and realize that there is a lesson being whispered very softly to me by this place, if only I can be patient and open enough to hear it.

One day while working in the garden, I observe a young couple who have come looking for a future wedding site. When they think no one is looking, they gently kiss while standing on the island of the Bodhisattvas, which lies in the center of the garden's pond. I can't help but think what a gentle symbol they are of the integration of masculine and feminine and the sacredness of this coming together. I feel that somehow they are pointing me toward a journey. I cannot escape the feeling that working alone in this untended place is only the beginning of a lesson I am being taught. Again, something calls me, and I strain to listen, but the only sound is the water of the koi pond lapping gently along the shores of the island, hinting at the promise of Nature's bounty and wet warmth.

I decide to continue at the garden when I can – I don't wish to join in the neglect that this place has suffered and continues to suffer – but I am frustrated by the sense that one person has so little impact. I decide that my nurturance must tip the balance in some way that can be felt by the garden and, by extension, the collective. If we are all parts of a greater whole, we must believe that even the smallest single shift in consciousness has its effect. As I touch the garden in my own small way, it touches me in small ways, too. I observe insects busy at their work, and I am fascinated by another world of which I'd taken little note before. The plants, neglected and unloved as they appear, seem to respond a little to my attention.

Like a small child with a dirty face and raggedy clothes, this garden needs me. I see its beauty, uncared for as it may be. Weeding seems to be what the garden demands from me, and so I oblige. On a hot morning in July, I try to find some shade and some weeds and proceed with my work. The voice in my head, the masculine one that believes I should be doing something more worthwhile and ambitious and that probably believes this should involve thinking, whispers that this is menial work. Another voice responds, "Dirty work is what you wanted, and it is worthwhile. You are caring for this little piece of earth that has been so neglected and ignored and, in doing so, you are caring for a little piece of yourself, too."

The realization dawns on me, as I recognize small changes in myself, that I need the plants as much as they need me. Weeding is, for me, the perfect antidote to my usual "thinking" state of being.

While digging around in the dirt, I find a luminous, black feather in the grass and wonder at the bird that left it there. I like that the feather is black, dark, shiny, and a little ominous. It reminds me of the other side of things, the dark, chaotic, earthy aspect of the feminine. These aspects need my attention, too. There is much I don't know, or have not cared to know, about the natural world, so much beauty and destruction, death and rebirth.

This is not just a concept. Feeling my hands in the earth points me to a connection and an involvement with the material world. The image of "my hands in the earth" turns out to be pointing me in a direction quite different than what I'd originally thought. The rain that kept me from my work, the discouragement that almost kept me from the garden, the circumstances that conspired to keep me from really getting my hands in the earth – all these, I recognize now, are faces of the feminine and of Nature.

I am again reminded of the deep wound to the feminine aspects of our very being, the wound that we all carry, men and women both. The voice of the patriarchy, so alive in me and in our culture, insists that things be perfect, thought out carefully, and that we always reach our goal. The garden teaches me otherwise. The imperfect has its own value. Ideas can marry with the material and create a third thing, something that words and rationality cannot describe. And perhaps, just perhaps, imagination is the bridge that joins masculine and feminine values, intellect and feeling, the material and immaterial, the earthy goddess and the airy god.

I've learned to keep dreaming, and that it's fine if those dreams don't always turn out the way I'd envisioned. Every day, I let go a little bit more of my habitual perfectionism and my thinking state of being. I do that in order to restore the balance in myself and also in the world. As each one of us embraces the forgotten feminine aspects of his or her being as individuals, we restore the balance in the collective, too.

That original image of putting my hands in the earth led me to work in the garden, but I could not have foreseen what would actually occur there. I believe this beckons us all to pay attention to our dreams and to the small gifts Nature has to offer. And, I believe this encourages us to appreciate it all, especially the weeds and the forgotten and unloved places, for the goddess appears in many forms.

....

Dr. June Stinchfield is a depth psychologist and a graduate of Sarah Lawrence College, the Westchester Institute for Training in Psychotherapy and Psychoanalysis, and Pacifica Graduate Institute. Her work is centered on the truth and validity of the imagination and in gathering circles of women in order to realize the power of the feminine to heal the world. She is a Jungian-oriented analyst with a private practice in northern Westchester County, New York, but considers her most important role at present to be a loving and playful grandma to her four grandchildren. She would like mothers and grandmothers everywhere to know that the loving and committed relationship they have with their children is one of the most important ways in which women save the world.

Nurturing the Feminine Spirit

By Alicia K. Vargo, president and owner of Pampered Passions Fine Lingerie & Post Mastectomy Services

....

Tragedies can occur at any time in one's life, and I believe how we overcome life's circumstances is a true test of the feminine spirit.

By the age of nine, my life was confusing, at best. My parents were divorcing after many years of being "out of love" and co-existing under one roof, and I felt frightened and alone. But, then, an inner voice whispered in my soul. Penelope (as she called herself) gave me a hug, warmed my heart, and spoke to me in a soulful, peaceful way. She told me this part of my life was temporary, that better years were to come, and to persevere through the trying times.

From the time I was five, I had wanted to name every animal I had as a pet (even fish) Penelope. When Penelope revealed herself to me, I finally understood why. To this day, Penelope guides me in every decision I make. She has kept me and my family protected from harm, and she has been my best friend: a constant hug of warmth, love, and kindness in the midst of loneliness and confusion. I feel her every moment of the day, and, through her, God.

My mother's health problems confined her to a wheelchair by the time I was five and so, from a very young age, I cared for her daily needs. That nurturance generated a sensitivity in me that allows me to care for others, sometimes even guess and meet their needs before they know what they need themselves. Penelope – my inner voice and secure peace that I have within me every minute of every day – gave me gifts to help protect and understand people in order for me to succeed in life.

When I was 13, my father had a massive stroke that paralyzed him and left him virtually incompetent. Life changed utterly. One day I was going to private school, the next I suddenly found myself in public school, without any of my prior indulgences. It was a difficult transition for me, particularly because I was an only child without a support system. My mother and father were too physically and emotionally disabled to support me, and I had an emotionally disturbed stepmother who had been jealous of the love I'd received from my father.

Thankfully, soon after my father's stroke, a kind neighbor took me into her home and got me out of the unhealthy environment to which I'd been subjected. Jane believed in me, which my soul needed desperately. Through her benevolence, Jane gave me back a piece of myself. She also gave me faith, love, and confidence. Unfortunately, she passed away from cancer within a year, and I was left alone again. Penelope was my lifeboat.

At 14, I found financial freedom by working double shifts at two different restaurants. (I had to lie about my age.) I enjoyed the spoils of my long hours, and I depended on myself and only myself. Within a year and a half, I had taken the GED test and graduated high school.

When I reflect on my life, I realize I've seen both sides of the coin – a spoilt, privileged existence and one of struggle and loneliness, without emotional or financial support. These experiences – and my unique perspective – contributed to my desire to nurture and take care of people. My adolescent trials also changed me. They gave me perseverance, confidence, and knowledge of the true extent of the human spirit. Through them, I became an assertive and independent person. I also learned how to create a good situation out of hardship.

I have worked very hard since my early teens. The restaurant business landed me my first job as a wine representative, which took on a life of its own. At the age of 32, I was a Senior VP of three liquor, beer, and wine wholesalers in the Colorado market. I also found myself on the Board of Agriculture, where I oversaw 22 wineries and was the Wine Advisor to the Governor.

One evening in the year 2000, just before I was to speak in front of 4,000 people at Coors Field, I realized I felt frumpy. I wanted to feel pretty "all under" before the speaking engagement, and I decided to go bra shopping to buy something to boost my confidence for the evening. At the store, an 18-year-old, size-two sales clerk came running up to me and asked if I wanted to be measured. When I said yes, she took me into a dressing room, measured me, and gasped, "You're a 38 around!"

"Yes, I know," I said.

"But, you're a shallow 'B' cup!" she exclaimed. "We don't have anything to fit you."

The wider a woman is around, and the smaller chested she is, the more shallow her cup size. Because of my size, I did not fill out the top of a bra as easily as other women with smaller bandwidths. I walked out of the store disheartened, without a pretty package under my arm. Instead of making me feel pretty, the bra shopping experience had left me feeling even more unattractive. Thankfully, Penelope was there. She reminded me how beautiful I was, that this experience didn't matter, and that the clerk's behavior was not my issue. Her words were a profound whisper of wisdom.

Feeling un-nurtured and un-cared for, I left the store and began researching the world's finest lingerie. This sparked a mission, and in 2001, I opened an online lingerie store called Pampered Passions Fine Lingerie. The mission of our business: Nurture the female spirit, no matter what shape or size a woman might be.

The business exploded. The store, and taking care of others, became my main focus. When we are out of our own selves, we lose our own day-to-day issues. Making women feel confident and good about themselves made me feel whole, which made me want to do more.

In 2003, I decided to expand the business by purchasing a retail store at Park Meadows in the Denver-Metro area. Shortly after the store opened, a woman in her 60s entered with fear in her eyes. I asked what was wrong, and she proclaimed she had just been diagnosed with breast cancer. She was scheduled to have a double mastectomy, followed by daunting radiation and chemotherapy. She was desperately searching for answers and direction, which, sadly, we did not have the means to provide.

After she left, I felt absolutely helpless, overwhelmed that I may have missed an opportunity to care for another. Though I wasn't quite sure what to do, I took immediate action to correct the situation. I always trust in Penelope to guide my decisions, especially when it comes to assisting women. I never wanted to turn away another tearful woman in need. With Penelope in tow, all pieces of the Post Mastectomy Department came together quickly. I soon hired a registered and certified orthotics and prosthesis fitter, approved with Medicare, so that we'd be prepared next time. I became a certified post mastectomy fitter as well.

Ironically, the first woman we fitted once the department was in place was a woman named Ruth – the same woman I wasn't able to assist a few months earlier. When I fitted her post-op, I was able to share with her that she was the inspiration behind our new services. Though I am not certain she understood the profoundness of her presence in our lives, it was important for me to tell her.

In 2007, as both our online and retail stores experienced continued growth, my husband and I purchased a warehouse. We also, after much consideration, bought a second house, with the intent of housing not only our business, but the women who worked for us in their times of need. Many of our employees were struggling with poor health, divorce, or money issues. We hoped to teach them financial and life skills and assist them in getting back on their feet, while they lived rent free.

The warehouse became a home, for varying durations of time, to those of our employees who were struck by the suddenness of life and required help in transformations and re-births of their souls. Even through the difficulty of the economic downturn, we strived to give these women in need a place to go and to provide guidance in matters of finance, life, and love.

One day, for a multitude of reasons, I wasn't feeling particularly pleased with my universe. Call it Mercury in retrograde. At work that day, however, I encountered three amazing and profound women who altered my definition of a "bad day" and forever changed my perspective on life.

The first was a pregnant, 30-year-old woman with a three year old in tow. The prior week, she had been diagnosed with breast cancer. She was due for a double mastectomy the following Monday, and she needed a post-op camisole. This looming deadline, which could reduce any other person to tears, seemed to this woman a mere inconvenience – life was going on as she'd planned to live it. Her courage was inspiring. I feel fortunate to be in the presence of women like this, to know that I may be able to make their lives just a tad more comfortable. Having a post-op garment that fits means there is one less thing for these women to worry about as they go through whatever stage they are in of their journey.

Most times they walk out less anxious than when they arrived, and I feel like I – and Penelope – have made a difference.

My next appointment was a 65-year-old woman. She had suffered financial destitution after she underwent a double mastectomy riddled with complications. She didn't have health insurance, and the mountainous debt that she'd taken on in order to save her life forever recalibrated the quality of her future. In spite of this obstacle, she remained certain that life is what we make it. Her story filled me with compassion and awe.

Finally, a 14-year-old girl came into the store. She had had one of her breasts removed, and she needed assistance to balance out her breasts underneath her clothes. She'd lost a breast before she even knew the full wonder of having two; yet this magical little girl, whom I see every six months now, was amazingly brave and confident. She possessed a maturity rarely seen in one so young.

By day's end, I was emotionally exhausted, yet there was a true profound feeling of wholeness in my spirit. These three amazing souls, who in the face of their genuine troubles remained optimistic and lively, made me recognize that my day was relatively easy. My issues in life at that moment, and forever after, seemed so miniscule.

Now, my favorite mantra is, "If this is the worst thing that happens today, you're doing all right!" I also have taken to calling all of my life's challenges "paper tigers." Paper tigers are ferocious and intimidating, and they tend to devour people, but really, they're paper and we can rip right through them if we attempt to do so.

Every blessed day of this life is a gift! Every day is a birthday (a glorious new day,) Valentine's Day (a day to love and accept love,) Christmas (a gift of life,) and an anniversary (a day to honor.) There's always something to celebrate! Live as though each day is special, for no reason other than that we are alive to breathe, to love, and to be adored, if we are so lucky. If you can't yet see your world this way, contend to make it as such! Remember: What's holding you back may only be a paper tiger, and all it takes to overcome it is a simple change in perspective.

. . . .

Alicia Vargo is the president and owner of Pampered Passions Fine Lingerie & Post Mastectomy Services, named "Bride's Choice" by WeddingWire and "Best Lingerie Store" by Intima Magazine. The company's mission to

"Nurture the Female Spirit," along with Alicia's caring nature, led her to win the Leading Lady Award from Denver's Ladies Who Launch, an annual award that recognizes exceptional female entrepreneurs. Alicia also has been named one of the Outstanding Women in Business by the Denver Business Journal and was a finalist in the 2010 Stevie Awards for the "Women Helping Women" award. She is the National Intimate Apparel Examiner for Examiner.com and has appeared in media outlets such as Fox, ABC, NBC, AOL Small Business, US Weekly, iVillage, and Cosmopolitan. Alicia travels the country fitting women for Dress for Success to help them feel confident "all under" as they take steps to improve their lives. She also dedicates herself to assisting women with post-mastectomy lingerie needs.

Alicia spent 25 years in the wine industry as an advisor to the Governor and served on the Colorado Board of Agriculture. Alicia enjoys spending time with her loving husband and business partner, John, and their four children, ages 18 to 22; reading inspirational and spiritual books; and sipping fine wine. www.pamperedpassions.com

I am Nurturing.

1. I nurture my body, spirit, and emotions through my thoughts, words, and actions.

2. I recognize that my needs are valid, and I actively take care of them or find ways for them to be tended.

3. I comfort myself in healthy ways.

4. I honor my wishes and my desires.

5. I spend time alone with myself every day.

strength ⚓

Catherine the Great

"I may be kindly, I am ordinarily gentle, but in my line of business I am obliged to will terribly what I will at all." – Catherine the Great

As Empress, Catherine the Great used her personal strength to transform Russia into one of the most powerful countries in the world.

....

Catherine the Great was born Sophia Augusta Fredericka, daughter to Prince Christian August of Anhalt-Zerbst and Princess Johanna Elizabeth of Holstein Gottorp. At the age of 16, Catherine converted to the Russian Orthodox faith and married the Grand Duke Peter of Holstein, grandson of Peter the Great and heir to the Russian throne. Though she despised her husband, Catherine wanted nothing more than to become Empress. An intelligent woman, Catherine understood from the beginning how to realize her goals. She worked tirelessly to win the approval of Peter's mother, the Russian Empress Elizabeth, and of the Russian people.

In January of 1762, Peter succeeded his mother as the Russian Emperor. He was an unpopular ruler, and frequently alienated the Russian nobility. On June 28, 1762, Catherine engineered Peter's removal from the throne and took power as Empress. She ruled Russia for over three decades and turned it into one of the most powerful nations in Europe. In the course of two Russo-Turkish Wars, Catherine crushed the Ottoman Empire and added 200,000 square miles to Russia's territory, which extended it to the Black Sea.

Catherine was a great patron of the arts and education, and she strived to modernize Russia in accordance with the Western Enlightenment. Her reign is widely considered to have been the Russian Empire's Golden Era. She shunned "the Great" while alive, and preferred to be called Catherine II. In addition to her achievements as a ruler, Catherine is widely known for her romantic entanglements. An independent woman, she took many lovers during her reign and promoted most of them to positions of high rank. When she deemed it time to move on, she rewarded the men with gifts of serfs and large estates.

Her great reign was brought to a close on November 17, 1796. Sometime that day, she fell ill. She died in bed within twelve hours.

. . . .

• Longest-ruling female leader in Russia

• Renowned for the revitalization of Russia

• Promoted the Russian Enlightenment

• Expanded Russia's borders 200,000 square miles to the Black Sea and into Central Europe

Harriet Tubman

"Every great dream begins with a dreamer. Always remember, you have within you the strength, the patience, and the passion to reach for the stars to change the world." – Harriet Tubman

Harriet Tubman's strength helped secure freedom for more than 300 people after The Fugitive Slave Act of 1850 left many escaping slaves in danger of being returned to their owners.

....

Harriet Tubman (born Araminta Ross) dedicated her life to the pursuit of freedom, not only for herself, but for everyone. Best known for her work on the Underground Railroad, she escaped slavery in 1849 and ran north to Philadelphia. Once free, however, she couldn't rest until those she loved also were free. In 1850, after the passage of The Fugitive Slave Act, she became a Conductor on the Underground Railroad.

Known as "Moses," Harriet made 19 trips from Maryland to Canada from 1850 to 1860. Upset with her success, slave owners posted a bounty of $40,000 for her capture. The State of Maryland added another $12,000 reward. She didn't let it stop her. Over the course of 10 years, Harriet moved more than 300 people from Maryland to Canada. She never lost a single passenger.

Other Conductors and freed men and women often talked about Harriet's strength. During one trip south, she pulled out her own tooth because it was slowing her down with pain. As a teenager, she was struck in the head with a lead weight while attempting to help another slave avoid punishment. This caused a permanent brain injury that led to headaches, seizures, and sleeping spells, which caused her to fall asleep at odd moments – even once under her own "Wanted" sign.

After Harriet's Conductor years were over, she served as a "contraband" nurse in the Union army. She nursed many black soldiers and newly escaped slaves to health. Later in the war, she served as a scout and a spy behind Confederate lines. In 1863, she became the first woman to command an armed military raid, the Combahee River Expedition.

Once the war was over, Harriet returned to Auburn, New York. Her final decades included work as a humanitarian, a community activist, and a suffragette. In 1897, Queen Victoria of England awarded Harriet with a silver medal. She died in 1913, at 91 years old.

• Most famous Underground Railroad "Conductor," 1850-1860
• First woman to command an armed military raid, 1863
• Made 19 trips from Maryland to Canada to rescue more than 300 people
• Never lost a single "passenger" on the Underground Railroad

⚓ Essays By Women

ℒearning through 𝒜cceptance

By Mary Ellen Ciganovich, author of "Healing Words, Life Lessons to Inspire"

....

It seems like my entire life could be summed up as a series of misperceptions, either of me by someone else or of someone else by me. The misperceptions began when I was diagnosed with petit mal lobe epilepsy at age six. Petit mal means "little bad" in French.

I remember my experiences as "fade outs." I wouldn't fall to the ground as in a grand mal ("big bad") seizure. I would just kind of turn off. Sometimes my eyes would close; sometimes they would stay open. Though I often felt dizzy after one of the episodes, my case was really very mild. Still, my family viewed it as a kind of death.

It was 1958, and most people – including my parents – viewed epilepsy from a place of fear. The day I was diagnosed, I found my mom and dad crying in the dark. I thought someone had died! When I asked my mother who had passed, she answered, "Oh, no one, sweetheart – we're crying for *you!*"

In that instant, everything changed. I went from seeing myself as my parents' cute, sweet, laughing, little girl to someone with a frighteningly large flaw. I felt completely unacceptable.

I was determined to be "normal," but my family constantly discouraged my efforts. I even was told I couldn't get married and couldn't have children. "At least you don't look like you have it [epilepsy]," my mother frequently said.

Even in my teenage years, my mother continued to act as if I were incapable of doing even the most routine things. She said I couldn't try out for the cheerleading team, and she discouraged me from trying out for Rich's Teen Board – a teen modeling position. But, I wanted to be a regular teenager so I tried out for both anyway – and made them! Through these experiences, I began to learn that with courage, strength, and a true belief in myself, I could do anything.

Before I went to the University of Georgia, my mother told me not to join a sorority and to keep my epilepsy a secret from everyone. "Just go to college, graduate in education, and get your teaching degree," she said.

I didn't listen. I knew I could do anything I put my mind to doing. I decided to join the Alpha Chi Omega Sorority, live in a sorority house, and get on with my life. But, something still held me back. I hadn't been able to shake my mother's admonition not to tell anyone about my condition. Even the man I was dating knew nothing about my epilepsy. I knew I had to tell him before he proposed marriage, but I couldn't bring myself to do it. Instead, I decided to try out the news on my roommate, Carolyne Frowein, or "Fro," as I called her. One night, while we were in our room, I gathered up my nerve. "I have epilepsy," I said.

"Okay," she said, "so what?"

I was astounded. *"So what?"*

"Evidently you have a very mild case," she replied.

It was true, I did. So why had I always been taught it was devastating? Obviously, Fro didn't think it was a big deal at all. She continued to accept me anyway.

It took me six hours to tell my boyfriend. After I was done, he said: "Is that all? I thought you were going to tell me you were dying or something."

Is that all? I couldn't believe it. Was I, perhaps, a worthwhile person despite my epilepsy? Was I, perhaps, deserving of love after all? Of course I was, but it would take me many more years of full-hearted acceptance before I believed it.

My boyfriend and I married and had one child, a daughter named Stephanie. When she was three years old, my biggest fear came to pass – she was diagnosed with epilepsy. I was distraught and angry. How could God do this? All I had ever asked from Him was to have a healthy child.

When I called my mother for support, she screamed, "I TOLD YOU – YOU COULD NEVER HAVE KIDS!" Then, she slammed down the phone.

Crying harder than ever, I called my mother-in-law, Hazel. In agony, I told her about Stephanie's diagnosis. I will never forget what she said: "Well, Mary Ellen, do you love her? Do you still love her?"

"Of course I love her!" I said. "I will always love her!"

"Then everything will be all right," she replied. "Don't worry."

I was shocked. How could Hazel accept such a diagnosis when my own mother could not? When I could not? But, she was right. I was proud of my daughter; she was (and is) a beautiful person, inside and out. A diagnosis of epilepsy couldn't change that.

Still, I could not shake off the guilt I felt over Stephanie. Terrified that all of my children would have epilepsy, I had my tubes tied.

Three years later, when Stephanie was six, we learned she had been misdiagnosed. She didn't have epilepsy; she was perfectly healthy! Shocking to me was that I hadn't needed to have my tubes tied, but the procedure had been done. It was too late to change it. Do I regret it? Really – I don't know. I never felt any less of a woman because of it. And while I have always been grateful for having Stephanie in my life, I believe everything probably worked out for the best.

Due to a combination of many factors, my marriage didn't last. After the divorce, Stephanie and I moved back to the Atlanta area, where I began life as a single parent. During that difficult time, I kept myself balanced by playing tournament racquetball. One day, during a tournament, I suddenly felt like a knife had pierced my right eye, all the way through to the back of its socket. My vision became impaired. I was frightened. What was wrong with me? I had never had these symptoms before! Unsure what to do, I called the match and walked off the court. I never played another tournament again.

To find out what was going on, I went to see an eye doctor, who sent me to an internist, who referred me to a neurologist. After all of the running around, I knew something was seriously wrong, but no one could give me any answers. Finally, my neurologist sent me for an MRI.

"You have MS," she said, after the results came back. "Multiple Sclerosis."

Luckily, I had never heard of MS and didn't have any preconceived notions of what it was like. *Okay*, I thought to myself. *You dealt with epilepsy; you can handle MS, too.*

The next day, I called the National Multiple Sclerosis Society and asked them to send me all the literature they had on MS. The year was 1986, and, at that time, all of the literature on MS was extremely negative. After I received the package, I became angry. I called the National MS Society and screamed at them, "How dare you send me such negative literature! This will not happen to me!"

The person on the other end said, "We hate to tell you . . . "

I never heard the rest of that sentence. I interrupted with "I hate to tell you!" and slammed down the receiver. Then, I took all of the negative MS literature and shredded it with my bare hands. I was so mad! The MS society was acting like my mother! It seemed everyone wanted to tell me what I could *not* do! I knew differently. I already had been here once. I could do it again! I would do it again! I was going to take control.

I studied MS, what it was and what it wasn't. I read every book about it, including "The MS Diet Book," by Richard Swank. The descriptions in the book taught me a lot about what was, and had been, going on inside my body.

Once I knew the symptoms, the question became: What could I learn from having MS in my life? From my past experiences, I understood I could approach my illness from a place of love or a place of fear. I also knew that if I chose fear, my fear would come to pass. So, I chose to approach my case with love and acceptance. MS did not happen to punish me. It simply happened so I could learn what I needed to learn and live the life I was meant to live.

After my diagnosis, I continued to teach middle school, be a mom, and date. Thankfully, even though I now had two diagnoses to deal with, I felt better about myself than ever before. There was a knowingness inside of me (I call it my God connection) that told me I was more of a woman now – even with MS – than ever before. I knew that if I felt good about myself as a vibrant female, someone else would, also.

Then, Peter Ciganovich and I met for coffee on a blind date. The attraction was immediate. We sat at the coffee shop and talked for hours. We were so comfortable with each other; it felt like we were old friends getting together again after a long time apart.

Once we began dating, I knew I had to tell him about my diagnoses before things became too serious. Since I played racquetball, I challenged him to a game. He had never played so I gave him 14 points and still won! That night I told him I had epilepsy.

"Okay," he said, "No big deal! Can't be very bad – you beat me playing racquetball."

A couple of days passed, and I still couldn't think of a creative way to tell him about the MS. Finally, I couldn't take it anymore. One day, I asked him to sit down. "I have MS," I blurted. "Multiple sclerosis."

He was silent. It felt like the longest second in the history of my world. Finally, he spoke. "Okay," he said. "I love you. Is there anything else you have to tell me?"

I was thrilled – thrilled he could love me and accept me just the way I was.

Thirteen years have passed since we got married, and we are very much in love to this day!

After all I have gone through, I have learned to be at peace with my mother. I believe she did the best she could. And, I am at peace with all those who have challenged me to love myself as I am. Both the National Epilepsy Foundation and the National MS Society have come a long way over the past few decades. Epilepsy no longer has the societal stigma it once had, and new treatments for MS are being found all the time.

I feel I was blessed to have gone through all of those misperceptions because I learned from the experiences that we women must learn to accept ourselves. We must also take control of our lives to create what we wish. Through our determination, we exemplify courage and strength to our daughters, our families, and all those who come in contact with us. We can use our intuition to share compassion with the world, and we can garner our awareness of faith through our expressions of love and forgiveness.

. . . .

Mary Ellen Ciganovich is an educator, author, and inspirational speaker. Raised in Atlanta, she was diagnosed with epilepsy at the age of six, and went on to attend the University of Georgia. She graduated Magna cum Laude in Education, and became a member of the Beta Sigma Chapter of the Alpha Chi Omega sorority. After graduating, Mary Ellen taught middle school for over 15 years. She also was instrumental in the existence of a two-mile-long nature trail in Danbury, Connecticut, and she created a book of environmental activities for teachers and students to use while on the trail. She was presented a key to the city of Danbury by the mayor.

In 1986, Mary Ellen was diagnosed with Multiple Sclerosis. She decided to use this to create her own picture of MS. Her book, "Healing Words, Life Lessons to Inspire," has been accepted for nomination for the 2012 Pulitzer Prize in Original Verse by an American Author. The book's teachings are words she lives by daily. She speaks to many groups on topics ranging from Awareness of the Self to Parenting and the Healing of Relationships, and has appeared as a featured luminary on "Inspire Me Today." She also speaks on the topics of Epilepsy and Multiple Sclerosis. www.askmaryellen.com

A Woman's Strength

By Sarah Hackley, editor at Absolute Love Publishing, published poet, and freelance writer

··

When I was in the fifth grade, my teacher asked each of us to write a biographical essay on the hero or heroine of our choice. I wrestled with the decision but ultimately chose Underground Railroad Conductor Harriet Tubman because I couldn't face the fear of writing about my mother. To me, both women represented unfaltering strength in the face of daunting and incalculable odds. Both pressed on when they felt they had no other option; both escaped brutality out of sheer will. But, one was a safe topic – and the other was my mother.

Now, almost two decades later and a little over six months after my mother's unexpected and somewhat unexplained death, I again am given the task to write about women's strength. It is a task I thought would be simple earlier this year, when I first contemplated the project. It is a task that feels heartbreakingly painful to me now, but one which may contain the power to heal.

My mother epitomized strength, or so it appeared to me for most of my life. Married three times – she was divorced once, widowed once, and then left for another woman – she also survived the death of two brothers, a brother-in-law, a father, two nephews, a niece, and a husband. She was a victim of countless acts of physical and emotional violence perpetrated by the people who were supposed to love her, yet she never considered herself a victim. She portrayed herself as a survivor.

As a child, I considered my mother a heroine. She was a quiet yet fierce woman, who believed the true power of humanity resided in the female sex. She believed we could do anything, and it showed. No matter the obstacle, no matter the defeat, my mother powered through. She rose from poverty to upper-middle class prosperity on her dedication, sharp wit, and intense intelligence. After carpal tunnel syndrome effectively ended her career as a paralegal (and her backup career of masseuse,) she returned to school in her mid-40s, and earned a Bachelor's and Master's in Information Science.

When her husband left her in the middle of her studies, she marched on – slightly angrier, much sadder, but determined to finish all the same. When he came back, she refused to take the blame for his mistakes and then did her best to forgive him. She overcame whatever life threw at her. The illnesses, the deaths, the heartbreaks – she simply added them to her already heavy burden and kept plowing. It was this relentless onward motion, this refusal to falter, that I considered strength. And, I emulated it for years.

When my first stepfather died unexpectedly of a heart attack and his children blamed my mother and me for not having saved him, I learned what I could from the experience (life is short – nothing is guaranteed – pain changes people,) and I moved on. When my uncles also died suddenly, separately, without warning or explanation, I added the lessons to the ones before, and I moved on. When I got pregnant in college, I decreed to make the most of it, and I pushed forward. Through episodes of domestic violence, rape, utter heartbreak, and challenging new beginnings, I upheld my mother's example: I pushed the pain aside, and I pushed through. And, I kept moving, kept pushing, until her death.

Suddenly, the one thing I had never been prepared for happened, and there was no place to push the pain. All the corners of my mind, all the compartments of my soul, were full. I found myself struggling to push a weight much too heavy to move alone. And, even more frightening, one I hadn't been taught how to handle. None of my old ways of thinking, of surviving, worked. Strength had always equaled function in spite of dysfunction – calm despite chaos. In other words, "containment." I imagined feminine strength as a quality that allowed a woman to survive anything without breaking. Yet, suddenly, I couldn't breathe, couldn't move, and I felt anything but strong.

I struggled to push the pain down long enough to function: to go to work, to smile at my daughter, to prepare dinner for my husband, to make it through the day. And, it worked, for a while. But, then, I'd be washing my hair or driving to the store, and the pain would rain down like a deluge. My hands would shake, the tears would flow, my breath would come in ragged gasps – and I would condemn myself for my inability to keep it together.

This won't work, I would think. *There are things to do. Buck up.*

And so, I would. The tears would stop, my breathing would return to normal, and I would carry on. But, those moments – when the pain pushed through and the world became impossibly large – began to come more frequently, until I found it almost impossible to experience any change in emotion without feeling on the verge of a breakdown.

At only 27, I felt lost. Weak. Alone. I imagined I had failed at everything my mother had taught me. *This shouldn't be so hard*, I'd think. *You should be over this by now.* But, I wasn't, and I couldn't think, or feel, my way there.

My internal life wasn't working, so I made the choice to get help. Little did I know that the help I thought I needed would be so very different from the help I would receive.

My therapist recommended a treatment called Eye Movement Desensitization and Reprocessing, which had been shown to help people who suffer from post-traumatic stress disorder.

"You've had a lot of trauma in your life," she said. "I think this could help."

At first, I was astounded. *I'm not traumatized,* I thought. *Life is hard, is all; mine no more than anyone else's.* But, she insisted I would benefit from it so I agreed to try.

The therapy was a revelation. It didn't work as intended, but it opened my heart to something I'd never understood before: I couldn't get inside my feelings, not even when I tried. I had built such a wall between my experiences and how I felt about those experiences that I was incapable of reliving both simultaneously. I could talk about my traumas, even walk through them, but I couldn't feel them. When I tried to bring it all together, when I tried to remember how I had felt, I disappeared in my own head. My to-do list took on grave importance. The book I read the night before filled my thoughts. Yesterday's article suddenly called out to be rewritten. I couldn't get inside myself.

Slowly, I came to the realization that my therapist was right; I had been traumatized, and I had internalized a single mode of survival – dissociation. In order to cope with my experiences, I had compartmentalized everything, including my feelings. I had shut my soul into a steel room deep within, a room so deep no one could find it. Sometimes, not even me.

I then realized that my method of "surviving" wouldn't work any longer. Sure, it allowed me to function in spite of dysfunction, but only because it kept me from feeling anything at all. Sometimes this is healthy; dissociation can enable us to withstand pain and loss under which we would otherwise break. It enables us to survive and pull through. But, a habit of continual dissociation – especially after the trauma has passed – leads to the shut-in feeling I was experiencing. While I imagined I was being strong in the face of pain, in reality, I was merely hiding.

Today, I can't say whether my mother was the heroine I imagined, or a woman caught in the struggle to survive life's pain. Likely, she was both, but our time together was too brief and too abruptly ended for me to ever know for sure. What I've come to realize, though, is that it doesn't matter; what she taught me about strength was so much more than how to *be* strong. Through her example, I have learned that women *are* strong – it is one of our most precious gifts. We can – and do – survive, even when we think we can't.

Feminine strength, I've realized, isn't about shutting ourselves off – it's about letting the world in. To heal, I can call upon the power of my feminine nature, that intrinsic ability to feel and learn in spite of – and perhaps because of – the pain. Past traumas are like old scars on tissue that never quite healed properly – they occasionally must be cut open, re-examined, and sutured anew. I can choose to open up and embrace all the pain I pushed aside over the years so that I can learn from it. Only after the feelings are let in, can they be let go.

It turns out that despite what I thought I had learned from my mother, her true lesson was how to learn from *myself.* And isn't that what mothers do? We hope to live in such a way that our children are better for having known us – and that they live in such a way so that their children are better still. Through my experiences, I am learning that strength includes acknowledging our emotions, and that sometimes falling apart is the bravest act of all because it requires we believe we have the strength to heal. As women, we live fully only when we feel. It is our emotions that make us brave, make us strong, make us wise. It is our feelings that make us women. It is our feelings – and our ability to learn from them and overcome them – that give us strength.

. . . .

Sarah Hackley is the editor for Absolute Love Publishing and its imprint, Spirited Press. Through both, Sarah provides individualized, comprehensive editing services to authors seeking to bring light and inspiration to the world. A passionate believer that the written word can change lives, Sarah is deeply honored to be a part of these projects. An author, ghostwriter, editor, and poet, Sarah also is writing her own books on the topics of financial independence and emotional healing for women.

Sarah's work has appeared on/in Code Blue Politics, OpposingViews.com, "Under The Bridges of America: Homeless Poetry Anthology," The Comic Bible, Crucible, On The Issues Magazine, Texas Family, Suite101.com, the Final Draft: Midnight Masquerade, and the "Austin Young Poets Anthology." Her poetry also was featured in an Umlauf Sculpture Garden exhibit. She has edited a number of full-length books, including "Love Like God" and the "Love Like God Companion Book." Due to an affinity for extreme temperatures and spicy foods, Sarah Hackley resides in her hometown of Austin, Texas, with her husband and daughter. www.sarahhackley.com

The Very Imperfect Journey of a Personal Trainer

By Michelle Hastie, a Certified Personal Trainer, Master NLP practitioner, and Master hypnotherapist

....

Personal trainers are supposed to have it all – strength, speed, and resilience. This is a misconception. The nametag and job description don't come with a certified perfect body, though the expectation that they do is certainly there. I should know.

Becoming a personal trainer had been the work of the divine for me. One day, I walked into the gym to be a kids' club attendant and was told that my outgoing personality would be a better fit in the gym, helping people reach their fitness goals. I was excited for the opportunity and never even considered the fact that I was a fairly inactive person who had never been very enthusiastic about working out.

One of the first things I heard after I became a personal trainer was, "You're a personal trainer? You don't look like one!"

I had always felt content with my 120-pound body, but that one comment was enough to trigger an avalanche of emotional insecurities, and severely damage the way I viewed myself. I was thin and small-framed, and though the woman's comment could have meant anything, I took it to mean that my body wasn't toned enough for me to be a personal trainer. Suddenly, I felt I wasn't worthy.

The next day, I asked my fitness manager what I could do to look more toned. I was told that I needed to count my calories and work out every day. It sounded simple enough.

Calorie counting was a completely different world to me. I had always eaten whatever I wanted, and I had only worked out because, well, I figured that's what adults did! After just one day, I realized that counting calories would be the hardest thing I had ever done. By 3 p.m., I had eaten all of my daily calories, and I was exhausted – too tired to even think about staying for a workout after my shift. Still, I had made a commitment to achieve the kind of body I thought I needed to be taken seriously as a trainer, and so I soldiered on.

I made the adjustments most people would make to stay within my calorie limits. I used artificial sweeteners, ate reduced-calorie frozen meals, and cooked with cooking spray – all of which went against everything my mom taught me about only putting *real* food into my body.

I was raised in a very health-conscious family. My mom taught me to avoid margarine, artificial sweeteners, and anything with MSG on a label. She taught me to watch out for high saturated fat and cook as much clean, real food as possible. My dad cooked fresh, healthy meals right out of our garden. When I made the switch to low-cal alternatives, I felt somewhat guilty for ignoring my childhood lessons on healthy eating, but I was determined to reach my goal.

I began working out with fellow trainers and found that I could model them quite well. Suddenly, not only was I walking and talking like a trainer, I was becoming a certified tomboy. All of a sudden, I had traded my heels for Nikes! I was claiming to love running like it wasn't a struggle at all. I was working out with the guys and letting them know I was strong and could lift weight they couldn't imagine.

Strangely enough, the harder I worked, the faster I gained weight – and it wasn't the good kind. I tried 2,000 calories, 1,800 calories, 1,500 calories, even 1,200 calories. I rode my bike to work, mountain biked on my lunch breaks, and strength trained at night. I attended boot camps on the weekend and ran five miles to the gym before a workout. I did hill intervals, followed by Plyometrics training, followed by a hike. I tried carb cutting, fat cutting, and all-out calorie restriction. The pounds continued to creep on.

I also struggled with overeating, binge eating, and dating. Who wants to go on a date with the girl who not only counts out every calorie on both plates, but also explains how many miles it would take to burn them off? Who wants to date a woman whose main goal is to be stronger than the guys? Who wants to date the girl who is so terrified of overeating that she avoids restaurants altogether?

Never in my life had I felt so uncomfortable in my body. As the pounds crept on, so did the stress. I felt trapped in a body that I didn't belong in and didn't know how to get out of, all while wearing a shirt that said "personal trainer." I put up a good front, but I was drowning inside – and I started binging to hold back the emotions that truly wanted to escape.

Food can control us, and that feeling can be absolutely overwhelming. Those who have never struggled with overeating and/or binge eating truly can't understand the complete lack of control I felt. My mind would find excuses to keep eating even when my body was screaming "no," and so I would continue eating. I couldn't stop. After the binge, I felt guilty, ashamed, and embarrassed, all of which only served to make me repeat the cycle all over again the next day.

Until one day when everything changed.

I was on my way to the mall to purchase another piece of athletic gear to add to my ever-expanding collection, when a woman in a black Jeep lost control of her vehicle and shot across the freeway. Before she hit the center divider, she hit the corner of my truck, which spun me around and caused me to fly across every lane of traffic – and get struck in each lane. The last car that struck me flipped me onto my side. After the collision ended, I quickly unbuckled my seatbelt and climbed out of the passenger door.

Barefoot and confused, I let two women who had seen the accident grab me, put me in their car, wrap my wounded arm, and call for help. I didn't feel pain; I didn't understand the damage of the accident until the next day.

Thankfully, I had met an amazing man (my current boyfriend) prior to the accident who picked me up and took care of me as I healed. He helped me lift my head when I didn't have the strength to do so myself. For weeks, I was couch-ridden and spent my days watching endless hours of television and sleeping. I ate whatever my boyfriend and his roommate gave me, and I didn't think once about the task of weight loss; the task of getting back to a normal life was too pressing. In the first month after my accident, I lost 10 lbs.

Nobody was more confused than me. Everything I had learned about calories made no sense. I was definitely eating more than I was moving so how could I have lost weight? I had started my own personal training business just two weeks before the accident, and my boyfriend helped me move around, pick my life up, and get back to work. There, I made it a priority to learn how I finally lost the weight I felt I'd done everything to shake.

I am happy to report that I did remove all of the excess weight, I didn't work very hard to do so, and I now eat all the food I want. My only workouts are hiking and yoga, and I traded my Nikes back in for my heels. So what happened?

I finally took time to nurture myself in a way that made me happy. I was finally relaxed!

Women today are more stressed than ever before! If we are under high stress and experiencing high anxiety, it might not be suiting for us to take part in extreme exercise. Before my accident, I was trying to fit myself into a role that wasn't mine to fill. I went from waking up with stress, to working out with stress, to eating with stress, to lying on the couch and not moving for several hours. On the couch, my body finally stopped producing all that cortisol that causes fat storage.

I also began taking care of myself, which is natural for women. We are nurturers. However, the first person we stop nurturing when life gets busy is ourselves! I stopped nurturing myself because I didn't believe I was worth it. I was disgusted with who I had become: why would I nurture a behavior of which I didn't approve?

Men reduce stress differently from women. Masculine energy usually feels more relaxed in a gym or with extreme exercise. Feminine energy often finds that to be pure agony; therefore, those situations often only serve to increase our stress levels. In order for me to release stress, I go to yoga or on a beautiful hike in nature. Other women release stress in their own ways – by playing with their kids at the beach, doing something artistic, or even having lunch with their friends.

I hear from a lot of women who are frustrated and upset because they believe men have it so much easier when it comes to weight loss. They say, "My husband starts going to the gym and drops 20 pounds! I have been doing that for six months and have lost two!" Remember, men and women are very different. We require more and less of different hormones and therefore have very different bodies. This means that if we attempt to lose weight like men, we are going against nature. There are some women out there who will have no problem losing weight in this manner, but the larger population will struggle with such a masculine approach to weight loss.

Losing weight and living in our ideal body means embracing our femininity. Play up your strengths! Join a seductive dance class, get into yoga, or find a Pilates class. Find movements that make you feel like a woman and allow you to relax in the way your body craves. Look for other ways to nourish your body and soul besides food, as nourishment is one of the ways that women relax. Use a bubble bath, a hot cup of tea, or a funny movie to feel nourished. When we feel nourished and fulfilled, we don't abuse ourselves. Those negative voices get quieter and quieter as the powerful feminine energy powers through.

The best way for us to release stress and allow our bodies to become what we desire is to decide what that body really is. What would you truly want your body to look like, if there were no women running around with 6-packs? Do you truly care if your arms are super toned? Get clear about what being a woman means to you and how you can embrace the qualities that make you attractive.

I have realized that I feel good when my body uses its strength to hold me in a grounding yoga pose and then dances through the flow of class. I love the feeling of dressing up and doing my hair and makeup. I love putting on a great pair of heels and standing in power. You will notice that what truly makes me feel good about my body isn't external, it's what is going on inside. Once we get this, we don't have to worry about it going away when we go on vacation, jump into the holiday season, or have a baby.

One of the complaints I always had was that I wanted to feel girly and dainty. I mistakenly believed that such a feeling required that I be small. When I found yoga and dance, I realized that girly and dainty meant confidence, sexiness, femininity, and radiance. And this, ladies, doesn't have a size requirement.

. . . .

Michelle Hastie is a speaker, author, and coach who works with overworked, stressed-out entrepreneurs to reduce tension around food and exercise, remove weight naturally, and return to freedom in a body that truly expresses who they are. This allows individuals to focus on their "genius work" and fully step into the truest version of themselves, ultimately creating the body and business of their dreams. Michelle's mission is to reach as many people as she can and help teach them how to live naturally thin and never have the stress or pressure to diet again. Michelle is certified in the field of food psychology and is a Master NLP practitioner, Master hypnotherapist, and Certified Personal Trainer. Michelle also was the featured coach for Shape Magazine's "weight loss diaries" for 2011, and helped writer Stacy Garay drop weight without dieting. Michelle is the author of "7 Ways to Lose Weight while Living Your Life," and she developed an audio series that helps people release weight naturally with little to no effort. www.totalbodyhealthsolutions.com

Achieving Authenticity – Right on Time

By Becky Sheetz-Runkle, author of "Sun Tzu for Women: The Art of War for Winning in Business" and speaker, strategic marketer, and martial artist

. . . .

Many women struggle with authenticity. Authenticity can't be faked. It can't be artificially forced. It's about being true to ourselves and to who we really are, and, while that sounds straightforward, it isn't an easy thing to do.

Achieving authenticity can be a very complex challenge, particularly in the business world where we're often implicitly told we have to emulate men's leadership, management, or interpersonal styles if we want to get ahead. While we may be able to learn a lot from the way men network within companies and play the "game," acting like men isn't being authentic to who we are as women. Authenticity for women is about understanding and leveraging our uniquely feminine attributes.

Journey to Authenticity through Martial Arts

My experience in the martial arts illustrates this. I've been a very active martial artist for over 20 years. When I began, I studied karate, which is a "hard style." The premise of hard styles is to use force to overtake force. You train to dole out as much power as you can. An attacker launches an assault, irrespective of his size. You stop him (or them,) and then inflict your own powerful force. That's the plan, anyway.

I trained in karate for many years, and I trained harder than anyone I knew. I was usually the first person at the dojo and the last person to leave. I was practicing while other students were socializing or resting. I pleaded with instructors for extra mat time. I attended as many seminars as I could. I frequently got together with karate friends for sparring sessions and training time. I watched as many videos and read as many books and magazines as I could. Because this kind of training required strength, and I lacked it, I started weight training regularly and seriously.

I trained like this for years. But, no matter how hard I trained and how many hours I put in, when it came down to action, I almost always got overtaken by the larger, stronger people. The bigger guys got the best of me, even ones who had only a fraction of the experience I had.

Something was missing. I was sure the problem was me. I committed to work harder.

Then, after over five years of training and after I'd earned black belts in two different forms of karate, I found another way. I discovered a system that wasn't a hard style, but was combat-centric. It was more self-defense oriented than the karates I had practiced previously. I began training in a system called Sho Bushido Ryu Jujitsu.

Unlike the hard styles, jujitsu isn't about stopping a powerful force. Jujitsu is about redirecting that force. Instead of using strength and size, the practitioner uses superior technique and sophisticated body mechanics to cause the adversary to use his own strength and energy to his detriment. I found that jujitsu was much more suited to my body type and much more practical for me.

But, proficiency didn't come easily. I often reverted to my default use of force on force, rather than unbalancing and outmaneuvering the attacker. I was frequently overpowered by the others, some of whom had superior technique, many of whom didn't.

It wasn't fair. But, it was the way it was, and I experienced a crisis of confidence. I doubted myself, and I frequently doubted jujitsu. Still, I continued to train and I was promoted through the ranks, ultimately achieving a black belt in jujitsu, followed by more advanced degrees. I never felt "ready" for these promotions. I missed that ethereal quality of confidence and legitimacy. I did all that I could to prepare for these promotions, but before, during, and after these tests, I still felt as if I had just squeaked by.

"Imposter Syndrome"

What I was dealing with is what many women (and some men) encounter in business and other pursuits. These people, including highly successful achievers, privately reveal their frequent self-doubt, fear, and insecurity. Researchers have found that even very accomplished women carry high levels of self-doubt that makes them feel like imposters. This phenomenon has been named "Impostor Syndrome."

For Imposter Syndrome victims, each new achievement exacerbates their fear of being discovered as a fake. These women believe they're getting by because of their contacts or because they've just been lucky, that it *can't* be because of their talent or skill. Going far deeper than self-doubt, this robs women of confidence and keeps them from recognizing achievements.

The Comfort Zone Versus The Pain Zone

Despite my initial feelings of self-doubt, I eventually grew into the confidence necessary to believe in myself. But, it took extreme measures, honesty, and time. Becoming proficient was a process, and it pushed me way outside of my comfort zone. It was painful at the time, but it taught me that we can either aspire to comfort, or we can really challenge and stretch ourselves. But, we can't do both. The path we take is up to us.

The following event reveals the stark contrast between comfort and growth. And, while no single experience caused me to arrive at authenticity, this is what it took.

I met my martial arts mentor, Uche Anusionwu, while we were undergraduates at Temple University in Philadelphia. I had been training for several years and was proud of my achievements. While Uche was the same age, he'd been training much longer and with an entirely different perspective. His approach was to get in and then disrupt, confuse, and destroy. My training had more boundaries and more rules. Not surprisingly, I was completely overrun by Uche.

I tried to view these sessions as necessary to improvement, but they were frequently demoralizing. One day we sparred in the foyer of my dorm room. In past encounters, I had always come away bruised, scratched, and dinged. This day was no exception. When you're losing the fight, and then losing your will to fight, you can feel the pain more vividly. Every thud and hum of every bruised shin, forearm, and knuckle echoes. The sting of every busted lip lingers. Each shot that gets through reminds you that you're losing. The painful sensation radiates deep beyond the flesh and limits your desire to launch a proactive response. But, when you're holding your own, adrenaline and enthusiasm mask the pain.

Uche feinted and set me up for a hip throw. Unable to counter, I anticipated being dropped hard onto the tile floor. The intensity of his execution and my fear of bodily harm combined as I let out a solitary gasping sob of fear. The impact was negated as he followed through and caught me as I fell. (People as skilled as he is don't hurt you unless they want to.) But, the fear and anticipation was anything but soft. I was defeated, again.

Comfort is a Choice
I wanted to stop training with this person who was so proficient at beating me. After all, if I didn't train with him, I wouldn't be reminded of my glaring weaknesses. We all feel better about ourselves when we aren't immobilized on our posterior, literally or metaphorically.

Or, I could continue, find out what I needed to do to even the odds, and grow. I chose option number two. After working with Uche for several years, I noticed a marked improvement. I was more aggressive, less fearful, more confident in myself, and better able to execute. Had I not left my comfort zone, I wouldn't have made the achievements I made in the years since. Today, I'd still be following a formulaic, predictable paradigm that didn't prepare me for the realities of combat. While the earlier days were tough, the impact these sessions had on my abilities and my confidence is beyond measure.

It Wasn't Easy, But It Was Simple
By leaving our comfort zones, we get knocked down and banged up, but it

beats standing still. The sacrifices may be great, but they're well worth it.

While this was a long and often very discouraging process, looking back I realize it was quite simple. I wasn't ready until I was ready, until I had duly prepared physically, mentally, and psychologically. At that point, I began to internalize the principles of what I studied rather than continuing to try to tack these principles onto my exterior. These principles and their execution became who I was.

Conditions must be right for this kind of self-acceptance. It only occurs when we've worked for and sought it earnestly. But, that alone isn't enough. It happens when we're ready, and not a moment before. It can't be decoded. It just is. If you believe in yourself and demand excellence at every turn, you'll grow into who you are to become. And, you'll do it right on time.

What caused this shift in attitude? It was a *process* that came from time and dedication. It came from watching my peers and measuring myself against them and from studying less advanced students and perceiving the stark comparison. Ultimately, it came from arriving at confidence in myself.

With a different way, in this case, the system of jujitsu, I found a path that suited me better. But, I only found this after a great deal of persistence and a heck of a lot of failure. It enabled me to be authentic, to be truly successful based on my unique attributes. And, most importantly, it enabled me to be these things when I was ready.

I believe the lesson for other women who are struggling with finding their right method and being true to themselves may also be in authenticity and timing. I'm not suggesting we stay back and wait for success or peace or happiness to find us, but I am saying we must be patient, while evaluating strategies that may be better suited for us, and give ourselves opportunity to grow.

Today, I look back at what I've been through and what I've overcome to be where I am today. I wouldn't trade any of my time in the pain zone for what I've achieved. I hold the rank of 9th degree black belt and Menkyo Kaiden, which is a license of total transmission in Sho Bushido Ryu Jujitsu. I run the Woodbridge, Virginia dojo and seek to help my students apply lessons so they can be true to themselves in the martial arts. The smart ones also apply this to many other aspects of their lives. When they're ready to, that is.

. . . .

Becky Sheetz-Runkle is a strategic marketer, speaker, and martial artist and the author of "Sun Tzu for Women: The Art of War for Winning in Business," called a "must read" by Today's Chicago Woman and recommended to Baseline Magazine's C-level readers. Becky is an expert on topics related to women in business and Sun Tzu for business strategy. An entrepreneur, she sold her marketing agency Q2 Marketing in 2011. She is a former Washington Business Journal columnist who has been published in the American Management Association's Journal, The Journal of Asian Martial Arts, The Glass Hammer, PRNews, GalTime, Yahoo! Shine, and MarketingProfs. Becky has spent her career measurably driving revenue for companies, with expertise in developing innovative corporate communications and marketing plans, exhilarating strategic messaging, targeted PR, and compelling copy.

Becky holds the rank of Grand Master in Sho Bushido Ryu Jujitsu and runs the Woodbridge, Virginia dojo. Her experiences versus much larger and stronger opponents have revealed much to her about overcoming adversity. Her hobbies include fitness, traveling, gardening, and animals (she's a big fan of pit bulls.) She's on a quest to find the world's perfect beer, which she thinks she's found in the Rochefort Trappist and Duck Rabbit's Milk Stout – but she's not a quitter. www.suntzuforwomen.com

The Mask

By Donna Visocky, founder of BellaSpark Productions and publisher of BellaSpark Magazine

. . . .

The day Kristi died, the doorbell rang at 5:30 a.m. Jarred out of a sound sleep, I jumped up, still in my pajamas, and glanced out the kitchen window. At the sight of the two squad cars, my heart stopped.

I opened the door to two police officers and a Chaplain. Before any of them could speak, I yelled to my husband, "Bob, get up! And, put some pants on!"

I wondered at that comment but somehow knew that morning would be a defining life moment. I didn't want it to be remembered with my husband standing in his boxers. I let the officers stand there on the front stoop; none of us said a word. Over and over, my mind screamed, "Don't let them in. Don't let them in! They can't say what they came to say if we don't let them in."

Bob appeared in the hall, and the blood drained from his face. "This can't be good," he said. And, then, he let them in.

"Do you have a daughter named Kristi?" asked the tall one.

Immediately, I knew my life would never be the same. My 21-year-old daughter had died in an automobile accident the night before, on her way home from an evening with friends, just a mile from her apartment.

Who was Kristi? She was a beautiful spark. Outspoken, compassionate, and tender with a strong sense of right and wrong – how that girl loved to argue! Struggling to fit in, trying to find her place in a world that didn't match her values. A child who gave her mother grey hair, not just a single strand at a time, but tufts of them all at once! Watching her grow up, I knew she would be an amazing woman, and I wanted to be more like her. She always spoke her truth, even when it got her into trouble.

After she died, I found a poem among her things that she had written in high school. She describes herself as a lover of music, dolphins, and her family; as feisty when she finds something to argue about; and someone who needs "lots of attention, my mother, and plenty of sleep." She wrote she feared losing me, being ordinary, and being alone when she grew old. She ended the poem by writing she would like to see her grandchildren be born, a woman become president, and to travel around the world.

I go back to work the week after Kristi died. I tell myself it is because I work in a small, two-person office and my new assistant is starting that day; someone needs to train her. I know the real reason is because I can't stand to be home in my empty house all alone with my thoughts. I pretend my presence is extremely important; pretending is a skill I learn quickly.

We paint the house that summer. My poor husband – it is my need to stay busy, not his; he covers the boards, as I paint the trim, wordless, one board, one window at a time, pouring my grief into each brush stroke.

When we lose someone we love, it's like a light goes out in our heart. When Kristi died, I felt the light in my soul would never shine again. Every day, I felt like I had to put on a mask in order to face the world. The mask was the only way to hide my pain and my grief. It was the only way I knew to make it through the day.

Then, little things started to happen.

I saw a butterfly and knew Kristi was with me and always will be a part of me … and the mask began to crack. My friend Rayno tells me that Kristi's smiling face pops into his mind and brightens his day. And, I realize she made an impact on people . . . and the cracks grow wider and the light peeks through, like rays of sun partly hidden behind a cloud. My grandson Nicholas tells me he sees Aunt Kristi, that "she is the brightest star in the sky." And, I know she is there to guide him … and the mask cracks a little more, until a faint light, my light, begins to shine through. My beautiful daughter Jenny gives birth to my new granddaughter, and I know she has been sent to me as a gift from God and Kristi to ease my pain. The cracks grow wider as I dare to allow my love and light to shine on this new child.

And, so it goes …

Slowly, little by little, the mask breaks apart, and I begin to feel the sun on my face again; the light in my heart shines. It may take years before I fully heal, but I begin to understand that someday, somehow, the mask will disintegrate entirely, and I will show my full face to the world once more. It will be a different face because I am different, but it will be my face, nonetheless.

How does one survive the loss of a child? The heart is resilient, I am told, and I guess I have to believe that. Even when I lash out in anger at a Universe that would take my child from me, I know I will survive this. We women are especially good at resilience. Perhaps we have an extra gene that allows us to endure terrible loss, tragedy, and untold atrocities. We are, after all, a wondrous garden, first growing babies and then growing faith. Maybe all that sadness becomes a sort of compost, gradually breaking down to create fertile soil from which spring seeds of hope for a more beautiful, peaceful world. It certainly seems so from the women I know.

My mother had resilience. She lived it in her own quiet way after losing her husband at age 38, raising five teenage children on her own, and again after being diagnosed with MS.

My friend Bonnie has resilience. She went to college at age 46 after her 17-year-old son, Billie, died. Now, she's a psychotherapist who focuses on grief and loss and works with parents who have lost children.

Wendy has it. It is for her daughter, Lacy, who was brutally murdered, that Wendy created the 2 Hearts 4 Lacy Foundation, which is dedicated to education, awareness, and prevention of violence. Wendy took her fierce determination all the way to the Colorado State Legislature to create something positive out of her daughter's passing, spearheading the passing of Lacy's Law.

Beena's daughter, Sonia, died of cancer at the age of 17. Before her death, Sonia started a non-profit called Peace is the Cure. Even though she is still fighting her own battle with grief, Beena has carried on her daughter's legacy, worked to raise money for cancer research, and promoted an end to war.

It's amazing how many women I have come to know who have lost a child. How is it I am a member of this club? I don't remember signing up for this, yet, here I am, at once both unloading my grief and carrying another's, with a group of women I never wanted to meet – strong women who share the load even when their own is overwhelming.

Where has my grief led me? On a soul journey I was not aware I needed to take. Shortly after Kristi died, I attended a Compassionate Friends meeting for parents who had lost children. A woman came up to me afterwards and said, "Your daughter was standing behind you all night, and she's a beautiful girl." She was a medium, able to connect with my daughter in ways I had yet to understand. What a wonderful gift to someone who has lost a loved one, to know that they are well and with you.

It took me a month to get up the courage to visit this woman.

"We agreed to do this," Kristi says in that very first reading with the medium. I am told it has more to do with my own soul's evolution than hers. "What was I thinking?" I reply.

So begins my journey.

I start by reading "how to talk to dead people" books. I learn and firmly believe my daughter is still with me, guiding me, whispering in my ear, wrapping her love around me always. Knowing she is with me in spirit brings some consolation, yet my arms still ache to hold her.

Slowly into my awareness appear other topics: spirituality, metaphysics, and new thought. Kristi's passing opened up a whole new world for me, and, as I search for answers, I realize there are others hungry to make sense of this great mystery – life and death, heaven and God. Perhaps we can take this journey together.

From my grief, BellaSpark Productions is born. It is dedicated to bringing the messages of many of the world's top spiritual visionaries and authors to people across the country through events, workshops, and BellaSpark Magazine. I chose the visionaries who had inspired me and opened my mind; I chose those who had incredible stories of their own. These were the messages I wanted to share.

People ask sometimes what motivated me to quit my day job and start my own business. "What have I got to lose?" I said. "I already lost my daughter. If I lose my house, what does it matter? It's just a house." Anything is possible when we realize most of the things we hang on to don't really matter.

And, Kristi – that beautiful spark – is my business partner, guiding me, nudging me to be a vehicle for change, helping create the world she always imagined, a world where children and nations are not bullied, a world where our differences are embraced and respected, a world at peace.

Is my life the same? No, it will never be the same. But, I still have three wonderful children who remind me every day how lucky I am to be a mother and a woman. Three beautiful and amazing grandchildren fill my life with joy.

The mask is pretty much gone now, though I have to admit there are times when the memories come, and I long to hide behind it so others can't see the pain buried deep in my heart, a pain that never quite goes away. But, I have traveled miles on this soul journey, and the path is getting easier. I see with more clarity, feel with more compassion, and enjoy little things more. I know without a doubt that life goes on and that we are never really separated from our loved ones.

I have learned to be resilient since the death of my child, to draw on an inner strength I wasn't aware I had. Today, I choose to face life head on; I choose to experience every minute of it, both the sorrow and the joy. This incredible play is my life, and I live it to the fullest. I let the mask go for good.

. . . .

Donna Visocky is the founder of BellaSpark Productions and publisher of BellaSpark Magazine. One of the top metaphysical and consciousness-raising organizations in the U.S., BellaSpark was named after Donna's daughter Kristi who died in an automobile accident in 2003. Kristi was a beautiful spark and passionate about creating change. It was her passing that propelled Donna on this soul journey. BellaSpark's mission is to be a catalyst – to stimulate, inspire, and embolden individuals and communities in their growing spiritual awareness by providing access to consciousness-raising ideas, people, and information. Donna has over 20 years' experience in non-profit work, business management, and event planning. www.bellaspark.com

I am Strong.

1. I respect my natural and trained abilities.

2. I appreciate the beauty of my body's feminine strength.

3. I am capable. I am intelligent. I can do it.

4. I respect and acknowledge my worries or fears – then leave them behind.

5. I honor every decision, every action, and every step as my best at the time.

trailblazing

Nellie Bly

"I took upon myself to enact the part of a poor, unfortunate crazy girl, and felt it my duty not to shirk any of the disagreeable results that should follow." – Nellie Bly

Nellie Bly's courageous foray into journalism gave a voice to the poor, the weak, and the incarcerated, and her trailblazing acts inspired women around the world.

. . . .

Elizabeth Jane Cochrane (aka Nellie Bly) was born May 5, 1864. When she was 18, Elizabeth read an article in the Pittsburgh Dispatch titled, "What Girls Are Good For." The article claimed women were only good for staying home and raising children. Elizabeth was appalled and wrote a letter of complaint to the newspaper. The editor was so impressed with her work that he hired her to write a column. At the time, it was deemed improper for a woman to work under her own name so Elizabeth Jane Cochrane became "Nellie Bly." Thus, one of the world's finest female journalists was born.

During her first years as a journalist, Nellie went undercover as a sweatshop worker and exposed unsafe working conditions and child labor. She then traveled to Mexico for six months and wrote on government corruption and the conditions of the poor, before she was ordered to leave. After she returned home, she received a trial assignment from New York World to get herself committed to the Bellevue Hospital on Blackwell's Island to expose the asylum's horrendous conditions. Her ten-day undercover investigation enraged the public, embarrassed New York City officials, and led to major reforms in the treatment of the mentally ill.

In 1889, Nellie set off on an adventure to circle the world in less than 80 days. The trip was meant to be both an enactment of and a race against the fictional character in Jules Vernes' "Around the World in 80 Days." No one had ever attempted to make the journey in that little time, and while the newspaper wanted to send a man, Nellie insisted on going.

She traveled from Hoboken to London, then on to Calais, Brindisi, Port Said, Ismailia, Suez Canal, Aden, Colombo, Penang, Singapore, Hong Kong, Yokohama, San Francisco, and back to New York. The trip took her 72 days, six hours, 11 minutes, and 14 seconds. Upon her arrival home, she widely became known as one of the U.S.'s most famous females. Her writings from her journey established her as an international heroine and changed the future of travel writing forever.

During WWI, Nellie spent four years in Europe as the first female war correspondent. Her behind-the-lines reporting provided a clear view of the war's human costs. After the war, Bly wrote for the New York Evening Journal until her death in 1922. At age 55, she died of pneumonia. The New York World eulogized her as "The Best Reporter in America."

....

• First female investigative reporter, 1887
• First woman reporter to have her own byline on her articles, 1887
• First woman to circumnavigate the planet unaccompanied by a man, 1889-90
• First person to travel around the world in fewer than 80 days, 1889-90
• First female war correspondent, 1914-1918

Amelia Earhart Putnam

"Please know that I am quite aware of the hazards. Women must try to do things as men have tried. When they fail, their failure must be but a challenge to others." – Amelia Earhart, in the last letter to her husband before her last flight

Amelia Earhart's trailblazing courage has inspired generations of women to accomplish their dreams.

....

Amelia Earhart is best known as the world's most famous female aviator. Her passion for planes started when she was 23, after she saw a stunt-flying show in Long Beach. She signed up for flying lessons just a few days later from a woman, Neta Snooks, and purchased her first plane within six months. In 1928, she became the first female passenger on a transatlantic flight from the U.S. to England. Though she quickly became world famous for her role, she wasn't satisfied. She wanted to fly the plane – not ride in it – so she immediately made plans to set out on a non-stop solo flight across the Atlantic Ocean.

Amelia's dream came true in 1932, and she was world famous once again. Into the early 1930s, Amelia's passion for flying trumped everything else. In 1935, she flew from Hawaii to California, from Los Angeles to Mexico City, and from Mexico City to Newark. Two years later, she planned her first around-the-world flight with three friends. A problem with the plane canceled the journey, but Amelia wasn't going to be denied. She immediately planned another trip.

On June 1, 1937, Amelia and Fred Noonan took off from Miami toward Central America. They flew east from Central America and South America to Africa, crossed the Indian Ocean, and touched down in New Guinea on June 29. In the final 7,000 miles over the Pacific Ocean, near Howland Island, something happened. Amelia's last communication was at 8:45 a.m. on July 3, 1937. Neither she nor Noonan was ever heard from again.

Amelia's legacy changed women's history forever. Her passion and bravery inspired women of all ages to pursue their dreams. In addition to her work as an aviatrix, Amelia Earhart volunteered with the Red Cross and worked as a teacher, a social worker, and an airline industry vice president. She also wrote two books and other articles about flying, and became an aviation editor for Cosmopolitan Times magazine. In 1935, she became the first female career consultant at Purdue University. She also served as a technical advisor to the Department of Aeronautics.

. . . .

• First woman to cross the Atlantic in an airplane, 1928

• First president of the Ninety-Nines, an organization of female pilots, 1930

• First woman to fly solo across the Atlantic, 1932

• First person to fly solo anywhere in the Pacific, 1935

• First person to fly solo both the Pacific and the Atlantic oceans, 1935

• First female career consultant at Purdue University, 1935

• First person to embark on an around-the-world flight over the equator, 1937

 **Essays By Women**

Finding Your Trail

By Rochelle Forrest, an author who fills tummies, minds, and spirits through empowering people to happiness and changing the world one person at a time

· ·

In the first half of my life, I played many roles. All were different and yet all were the same. In each, I served as an invisible support. Daughter, mother, wife, or nurse – I was always trying to clear someone else's path. Like many women, I felt the need to rescue everyone but myself, to whom I never gave a thought.

Then, one day, I had an awakening. Like many awakenings, mine came at a time when my energies – mental and physical – were most depleted. I was exhausted from letting myself be pulled in a number of directions and from ignoring my own needs. But, it is often at these times, when we are at our lowest, that we are most open to divine guidance.

On that day, as I sat in the park, I began to look for answers to get myself moving in the direction I knew I wanted to go. Ever since I had started working as a nurse, I felt my heart's purpose was to inspire others to lead the lives they had always dreamed of leading. But, I wasn't there, yet – in fact, I was a long way off from doing what I felt I was meant to do.

Suddenly, my heart opened, and I realized that life is like an oxygen mask on a plane – we must save ourselves before we can save or help anyone else. All the love in the world won't make up for a good, solid example to follow. I longed to help others realize their dreams, but how could I teach people to discover their own paths, to translate their inner fire into light for the outer world, until I'd done it myself? How could I teach others to be the stars of their own lives, when I hadn't played the leading role in my own?

I knew I had to change my perspective. It was time for me to stop living life secondhand. But, as many of us know, it is much easier to say it is time to find a new path than it is to actually go out and find one. Most of us live life on a treadmill; we put in a lot of effort, but we never get anywhere. I didn't want to live like that so I started to look for signs to guide me in finding my new way, and I discovered the earth's natural rhythms. The seasons became significant in how I thought.

Winter became a time to hibernate, to think, to rest, to plan, and to let things build quietly. Spring was the time to plant, to implement new ideas, to start new projects, to burst forward with renewed energy. Summer was the time to tend and watch and make certain all was progressing toward a bountiful harvest. Fall was the time to reflect on the year's progress, to shed the things and ideas that didn't work or didn't contribute to the year's goal. Working with the rhythms of the natural world, instead of against them – as is so easy to do in our man-made technological lives – made me see things more clearly. It gave me time to process, instead of always rushing forward.

My inner light became brighter. My senses – sight, hearing, taste, touch, and smell – were awakened. I started to listen to my body and my inner voice. The seasons led me back to my heart, and I was finally able to allow my past hurts to come to the surface to heal. My inner trail began to blaze, and I suddenly understood I wasn't the only one who had lost her inner light by neglecting her own needs.

As I became crystal clear in my vision, I wrote it down. I started to work on a map for the second half of my life. I developed a vision book, vision boards, and signs – everything that could point me toward my destination. It was like setting my internal GPS to guide me to my holy purpose. I knew there might be detours, unexpected weather, and even some wrong turns, but I was determined to get there no matter what.

I worked on my physical body, health, endurance, strength, flexibility, and balance. My external presence reflected my internal presence, and my inner presence reflected my outer presence. When I felt fragmented, I stopped, breathed, and believed. I looked at my final destination and tweaked the course as needed. I came to know that everything I experienced was for my highest purpose.

When I had made progress but still didn't know exactly what to do next, I began to question God. Every day for four months, I asked, "What am I to do with all of this life experience?" Each day, I sat quietly and listened for the answer. One day, I woke up and wrote a children's story, "Shelly and the Circle of Light." Shelly is a lightning bug, who doesn't know she flies and doesn't know she shines. The story is her journey to find her purpose, and, through it, my own platform took flight. Suddenly, I was very clear and concise about what my personal message was and what role I was to play in this world. I was on fire.

Now, in the second half of my life, I no longer play the supporting role. Now, I am a trailblazer, developing tools that can assist each of us in finding our inner paths.

We each have experienced pain in our lives, and something within us drives us to fix it, to change it, to stop it, to do anything to make it better. My system enables us to feel that pain and to understand the force behind it. Instead of hiding from, ignoring, or running away from our pain, we can transform our pain into power. As we live in our power, we connect to our greater good, which goes with our purpose.

I believe that whatever is in our hearts – love, light, song – comes out when life squeezes us. This is true for both positive and negative feelings. If you have hate, jealousy, or anger in your heart, then when life squeezes, you will get domestic violence, road rage, and bullies. If you have love, acceptance, and compassion in your heart, you'll get unconditional relationships, peaceful interactions, and the kindness of strangers.

Spirit knows no limits, but we must trust in the process. Begin with you. Take in a breath, inspiration, in-spirit. Feel what is around you. What is coming up? Be present. Absorb your surroundings, and know that everything in your today stems from your thoughts of yesterday. If you don't like a result in any area of your life, change! We each are encoded with a purpose for this lifetime. Each of us is necessary. It is time for us to share our light.

I believe that as we awaken our gifts, we are to share those gifts with others. Share your vision. Help people to see. Have courage. Look around for models with similar values. Own the traits you have within. Each of us is uniquely designed and encoded with our individualized gifts, which is why we need to work together. Alone we only have our gifts to share, but together, we can achieve miracles.

In the spirit of sharing, I offer you these thoughts from my experience . . .

Not everyone is going to "get" you, and not everyone has to "get" you. As you begin to forge your own personal path, some people will fade away from your path and new ones will join you. This is necessary. Let it happen.

What is your "why?" Make a list of what you value. If you know why, then the "what?" and the "how?" will be much clearer.

Create space for daily listening. Allow whatever guides and inspires you to give you those intuitive nudges that keep you on the right path.

Have a support team. A circle of caring people who support, encourage, and believe in you, according to your needs at the time.

Have an inner knowing that you will accomplish your why, no matter what.

When you believe, you achieve. It is one of life's truths.

When you feel down, take a moment to breathe, re-set, re-frame, and move. A new idea will present itself.

Don't attach to the outcome. Just keep moving in the direction of the goal.

Be thankful for the process, and remember this is your journey. It's not about a destination. It's about how you get there, what you learn, and whom you help along the way.

Ever since I discovered and understood my own "why," I have awakened each morning enthusiastic and joyful to have another opportunity to express my spirit and make a difference in the world. Now, I am working with groups to help adults on the path to better physical health. I also am developing educational seminars for children based on the lessons from "Shelly and the Circle of Light." My purpose – my gift – is everything to me.

Now is the time to lighten up! Take control. Awaken to your life. Acknowledge what is working and what you would like to improve. What makes you happy and brings you joy? When we are living with heaviness in our hearts, it is very hard to open ourselves up to life and love. Women lead with our hearts, not our heads. We think inclusively, and our first choice will always be to find a consensus rather than dispute a question. This puts us in the strongest possible place to nurture the intuitive sparks that become genius and passion. As we find and walk our own paths, we can walk beside others and encourage them to seek their own light. We can build a strong community in which we each can participate in making the world a better place – one enlightened, fulfilled, strong person at a time.

Author **Rochelle Forrest** is a passionate and spirited holistic health coach dedicated to helping others heal their lives. A Registered Nurse for over 27 years, she holds a Bachelor of Science in Nursing, a Master's in Science in Management, and the most important designation of all, L.E. (Life Experience.) Rochelle recently found one of her childhood drawings. She had painted that she wanted to be a mom, a wife, and a nurse. She had unknowingly made her first vision board when she was five years old. This reinforced her belief that acting intuitively is the best way to strengthen our inner guidance system and that reigniting this guidance system is the key to good health. Rochelle, unwittingly and intuitively, started coaching people about their health and lives at her clinic. Eventually, the doctor told her she should start a coaching practice because that was what she was doing!

As part of her dedication to healing, Rochelle became involved in children's charities. Her book, "Shelly and the Circle of Light," gave Rochelle a way to fill the hearts and minds of children even as she worked to help support them in more practical ways. A portion of the proceeds from every book is donated to support children in need. www.createhealthnaturally.com

Blazing a New Trail for Healthcare

By Dr. Katie McCorkle, author of "A Balanced Heart: 10 Weeks to Breakthrough" and founder of Balanced Heart™ Healing Center, a nonprofit integrative health center for mind, body, and spirit offering care unconditionally

· ·

"Two roads diverged in a wood, and I,
I took the one less traveled by,
And that has made all the difference."
- Robert Frost

I always have been an adventurous person, drawn to places others feared to go. Whether it was voicing a different opinion, traveling alone, or caring about the forgotten, when I came to a fork in the path, I often chose (like Robert Frost) "The Road Not Taken." From the early age of 11, I knew that my reason for being on earth was to heal relationships. As an adult, I believed I had embraced my calling when I became a child and family psychologist. I had a relatively easy and comfortable middle-class life, good friends, a private practice, and a backyard I enjoyed as my own Garden of Eden. I trusted that God was leading me someplace good. After all – what more could I want?

Then, ten years ago, I unexpectedly received an invitation to be interviewed on the radio. It was my first time on air, and I wasn't sure what to expect, but it was so much fun that my feet didn't touch the ground for about three days afterward. I did call-ins on two more radio shows before the debut of my own half-hour weekly show four months later.

During my first show, I spoke about our dreams for our lives ... how they are conceived, nurtured, grow and change, and finally are birthed into the world. Of course, we also talked about how dreams can be denied, forgotten, or put away for later and the consequences of those choices in our lives as well. About halfway through the show, I heard myself say that I dreamed of one day speaking to a million people on the mall in Washington, D.C., and of inspiring them to go and do great things in the world. WHOA! I thought. Where did that come from? I had never dreamed of doing that! I couldn't even imagine it. Thankfully, the kind person running the board quickly cut to a commercial while I regained my composure.

About that same time, my coach began urging me to "write the book." I had never thought of becoming an author and had no idea what my book might be. Nonetheless, I began keeping a journal of whatever I felt inspired to write in hopes of discovering my book. Six years and many hundreds of pages later, I finally realized in a flash of brilliance that the book was to be a guided journal that would offer people the tools and strategies that had helped me along my path. Within ten days, the essence of the book poured through me and onto the page.

Those years of journaling also saw me through the preparation for blazing a new trail in healthcare. I had the opportunity to preview and practice new skills that would be necessary later. There was a great deal of networking with other women (and men) who were also searching for their purpose in life and a better way of responding to people's needs. We shared stories of our ideas, successes, frustrations, and challenges, and we supported each other on our way forward. I taught classes and led seminars on love, relationships, and birthing dreams. There were more recording and media projects, potential partnerships, and always more questions than answers.

As suggested by the poet Rainer Maria Rilke, learning to love the questions without needing to know the answers was an essential part of my spiritual formation during that time. It helped me move beyond my ego's need to know or control or "be right." It helped me learn to let go more easily, to consistently cultivate an attitude of curiosity, and to live into the questions. Through this process, I learned to humbly open my heart and entrust the outcome to God.

Every now and then, I paused to reflect on the journey and the process. During those precious moments, I saw glimpses of how I was changing, and how the work was strengthening my faith and increasing my confidence. Helping others manifest their dreams was as much of a self-awareness tool as anything I did for myself. I still didn't know what my dream was, but my passion for pursuing it was off the charts!

One day, a woman who had been in one of my "Birth Your Dream" classes called to ask if she could take me to lunch. She said she had been on an amazing journey and had a burning desire to give back but no clue about how to get started. I don't recall what we discussed at lunch that day, but I came away knowing that I wanted to provide a physical place and a support structure to make it easy for her, and others like her, to share what was in their hearts to share. It was then that I finally discovered my own dream ... helping others to manifest their dreams.

Two months later, a group of 20 people came to my home to participate in a visioning ceremony for Balanced Heart™ Healing Center. Afterward, one of the participants, the CFO at a Pittsburgh business, sent me a long, effusive email about what an incredible vision the Center was. He laid out how to get started in order to attract the next several levels of support and concluded by saying that, before we knew it, we'd be bringing $10 million each year into the local economy. He exploded my notion of what I had agreed to do, for I was unaware that I'd said yes to something so big! Even then, I could not see the whole vision of what Balanced Heart™ Healing Center eventually might become. Miraculously, his email didn't frighten me; it merely opened my eyes to the possibilities.

From the very beginning, Balanced Heart™ Healing Center was a vision of sustainable community-building and shared purpose, a vision of a world where every person has affordable access to the healthcare resources they need, a world where there is enough love and respect for everyone to thrive, a world where conducting business is an act of love toward others and oneself equally. The community of people who support Balanced Heart™ Healing Center in ways large and small focus upon the good we can create for ourselves, each other, and the planet we share. This is a vision I love and believe in, a vision that came alive in me at that moment.

Like parenthood, creating something innovative is the greatest job for which we receive no training (unless we pay attention to what has come before.) For better and for worse, we all learn about parenting from what our own parents did. As adults, we often base our views of what we are capable or incapable of doing upon what we have done before. Reaching out for something more, or behaving in new ways, requires a leap of faith into the unknown.

Balanced Heart™ Healing Center is now building a bridge between the way healthcare has been practiced in the past and the way it will be practiced in the future. Using as our starting point the power of a self-aware mind to create health by activating the body's own inner resources, the power of food and lifestyle choices to heal, and personal responsibility, Balanced Heart™ Healing Center is an integrative health center serving people unconditionally, regardless of their insurance status or ability to pay. We are committed to living the 10 Principles of Unconditional Love that guide our interactions with each other, our clients, and other stakeholders.

Sadly, most people in this country believe that affordable, sustainable healthcare for all is not possible. We say it is. I always have believed that there are enough open-hearted healers of all kinds that if we had the organizational and technological resources to match those healers with people in need, all people could have access to healthcare resources. Balanced Heart™ Healing Center aims to demonstrate the viability of this belief, first in the Pittsburgh, Pennsylvania region, as an example for others to follow.

I know this is possible because I have been treating people unconditionally in my own psychology practice for more than a dozen years. At times, up to 50% of my clients otherwise would not have had access to the mental health services they needed. The challenge was to design the business model for a group practice that allowed all stakeholders – providers, clients, insurers, and the government alike – to contribute as they are able and have their needs met in a financially sustainable way.

It was important to find a way that would allow everyone who wanted to be involved to contribute (and receive) as a partner, client, donor, or volunteer. We wanted to support people who didn't have insurance coverage for the healthcare services they needed and give them confidence in their capacity for self-support. Our vision included young people at the start of their careers, as well as those struggling to build businesses in complementary and alternative healthcare fields who have been shut out of the insurance reimbursement system. We wanted to include efficacious new healing technologies and energy medicine that may not yet have reached full mainstream acceptance. For a while, my brain hurt as I developed a business model to meet all those needs with our existing resources, but ultimately a unique solution emerged.

Now, ten years after my first radio interview, my dream is coming to fruition. The foundation has been set, the book is published, and the media promotion is underway. We haven't yet inspired a million people to go do great things in the world (at least, not that we know of,) but both the movement and our visibility are growing.

Healthcare providers, committed volunteers, universities, and veterans alike have joined hands with me to launch Balanced Heart™ Healing Center's clinic, which is now working toward becoming Pennsylvania's first state-licensed, holistic mental health clinic. Together, the mother of the vision and volunteer "midwives" are birthing this dream to save the world. I can hardly wait to see what the dream becomes as it takes on a new life of its own!

. . . .

An innovator educated at Stanford University, the University of Pittsburgh, and Harvard Medical School, **Dr. Katie McCorkle** is a holistic coaching psychologist with decades of experience. She developed award-winning programs for drivers under the influence of alcohol or drugs and for learning-disabled delinquents. She also was part of a team that developed the first program for adolescent sex offenders in Pennsylvania. In the media, she has hosted her own radio show and podcast; been interviewed on stations throughout the United States, Canada, and England; and contributed to the development of transformative programs for divorced, separated, and bereaved individuals.

Dr. Katie, as she is known to her clients and in the media, is the founder, CEO, and Chief Healing Officer at Balanced Heart™ Healing Center, a 501(c)(3) nonprofit integrative health center for mind, body, and spirit offering unconditional access to care. Balanced Heart Coaching, the spiritually centered coaching program Dr. Katie developed, is a system of tools and strategies for living life in greater consistency with one's spiritual beliefs. Her guided journal, "A Balanced Heart: 10 Weeks to Breakthrough," walks people through how to use these tools and strategies successfully. www.balancedheart.org

Trailblazing

By Shannon Miller, founder of Shannon Miller Lifestyle: Health and Fitness for Women and the most decorated American gymnast in history

....

Oftentimes, trailblazers have no idea they are blazing new trails. In my case, I was simply doing what I loved. I was passionate about becoming the best gymnast I could be and accomplishing the best I could each day – and the truth is, I don't think the records I broke or the titles I earned began to sink in until at least a decade after I finished my Olympic career. Even now, I'm not sure I can truly wrap my mind around the enormity of these accomplishments.

I had a modest childhood. I grew up and trained in Oklahoma, where I followed my older sister into the sport at the age of five. At the time, I had no great ambitions to blaze a new trail in United States gymnastics history – I had never even watched gymnastics on television! More than anything in the world, I simply wanted to be like my big sister.

Watching my sister and learning from my mother and other female role models helped propel me. My mother is athletic and intelligent, and she taught me early on that I should never set limits on my potential. If I worked hard and remained dedicated, I could do or be anything in life. I carry that lesson with me still today.

For most of my career, I was not the most talented athlete in the gym. In fact, for the first several years of my competitive career, I'm not sure I stayed on the beam during a competition. It took me longer than the other girls to learn critical skills, and at times it felt like I spent my entire career learning how to come back from defeat. But, these challenges created determination and a work ethic in me that rivaled those of more seasoned athletes. It was these qualities that allowed me to push the trail just a little bit further each time I stumbled.

And it's this aspect of women trailblazers that I believe is so critical. What is trailblazing, but simply going a little further than the women who came before us? Isn't that part of our destiny – to follow each other, lead each other, and lend a helping hand to those behind us? This circle, this process, is what gives us the strength and the capability to move ourselves forward continually.

Sometimes, it is life itself that pushes us further. In 1992, I landed arms-first from 10 feet in the air while training on the uneven bars for the Olympic Trials. I dislocated and broke my left elbow. Here I was, at one of the most crucial moments in my life up to that point, and, in the span of three seconds, my path changed.

Yet, something that I might have viewed as "bad" ended up being a catalyst. I realized everything could be taken away in the blink of an eye, and this completely focused my every thought and every action from that point forward. Not only did I make the 1992 Olympic Team, I walked home with more medals than any other American athlete, from any sport! I had moved forward on my path because of a bump in the road.

Then, while competing at my Olympic qualifier in 1996, I faced yet another setback. I fell during my first event, the balance beam. The saying was, "You can't fall and win." However, what I had learned was that when you fall, you get back up, you minimize your mistake, and you KEEP GOING.

I went on to perform some of the best routines of my life in the other events, and by the end of the night, I proudly stood atop the first place podium, securing a spot on my second Olympic Team. Sometimes, you can fall and win. Maybe in life that's the only way you can win. You fall . . . and then you get back on the beam.

We truly learn more from our challenges and our mistakes than from our successes. Falling didn't rattle me as much as it did some of the other athletes because I was used to it. I had been falling for years! I was also used to picking myself up and putting the past behind me.

I love the quote from Wayne W. Dyer, "The more you see yourself as what you'd like to become, and act as if what you want is already there, the more you'll activate those dormant forces that will collaborate to transform your dream into your reality."

In short – if we can see it, we can do it. I think this is an important truth, particularly for women. As we are blazing trails and moving toward places other women have never reached before, we must first imagine ourselves in those places; we must activate and unleash the dormant power of our subconscious.

When I was a child, my coach often encouraged us to write down our long-term goals. I wrote, "I want to compete at the Olympic Games!" The summer of 1996, I had my second chance. My team, the "Magnificent Seven," as we would come to be known, walked into the Georgia Dome to 40,000 screaming spectators. Somehow, we knew it was our night; it was a magical evening I will never forget.

I think back to that time and wonder how I got through those tough days of training – seven hours a day, six days a week. It was the plan, the goals I had set in place, that kept me motivated through the injuries, the pressure, and the tedious repetition. Through it all, I held onto my vision. By the end of the 1996 Olympic Games, we proudly stood atop the podium, and received the first Women's Gymnastics Team Olympic Gold Medal in United States history!

After I retired from gymnastics competition, I focused on creating the life I wanted for myself. Both of my parents had instilled in me that education was the key to success and would lay the groundwork for whatever I wanted to pursue in life. I went to college, then to law school, and eventually married and started a foundation to fight childhood obesity. In 2009, I added yet another role: mom. While expecting our first child, I decided to launch my company, Shannon Miller Lifestyle: Health and Fitness for Women. I wanted to open the lines of communication for women and share my passionate advocacy for women's health. Life was great!

Then, it was the holidays, and my schedule was crazy. My little boy was becoming mobile, and I had program launches for my foundation and company on the horizon. I realized I was going to be out of town on the date of my scheduled yearly physical exam. When I called to reschedule, I had a nagging feeling. Instead of canceling, I followed my gut and took the first appointment available – that very morning.

I had a seven-centimeter tumor on my left ovary.

Life quickly snowballed into a whirlwind of tests and exams. Soon, I was hearing words like "mass," "malignancy," and "cancer." My world stopped. Everything I thought was so important suddenly seemed trivial.

When I went into surgery to have the tumor removed, I still didn't know whether the tumor was benign or much worse.

At first, there seemed to be great news. While the tumor was indeed a malignant germ cell tumor, a form of ovarian cancer, it had been caught very early, and the prognosis was positive. But, a couple of weeks later, I got the call: the tumor was a higher-grade malignancy than originally thought. The typical course of treatment would be nine weeks of very aggressive chemotherapy.

That conversation was a game-changer. My husband and I had been hoping to announce a second child on the way. Instead, we were discussing cancer and chemotherapy.

In gymnastics, I had never worried about the other competitors. I would win or lose on my own terms. My goal was to prepare and compete to the best of my abilities. Many times, we can win a competition before we even step on the floor. With cancer, I applied this mentality: I decided to prepare, dig in, visualize, keep moving forward on my trail, and do the work.

Cancer focused my priorities like never before. I had a new long-term goal: to live. I wanted to be a mother to my son, a wife to my husband, an advocate for women. Sometimes it takes a crisis to get us back on track, or to move us forward in a new way. Thankfully, I already knew this.

I knew I had to remember to look at the bigger picture. The nausea would eventually pass. I had to move forward. I thought about the tough times I'd been through in my life. Each of them had made me a stronger person. I reminded myself that God never gives us more than we can handle, and that with His Grace we can overcome all obstacles.

During those first nine weeks, I relied heavily on the Olympic mindset that got me through tough times in my career, but I also relied on communication with other women survivors. They helped me keep a positive attitude on some of my darkest days, and I think, in part, it was the strength of those women that helped me overcome cancer. Women seem to have an innate strength when it comes to helping others, a soul sisterhood.

I remember when I lost my hair. I was terrified my son would be scared of me. I had nightmares of him crying in fear of "bald Mommy." Hair is a huge part of our identity as women, and for me, the loss was such a reminder of illness, such a symbol of cancer. I voiced my fear to a friend, and she said, "Shannon, if you're not comfortable with how you look, your son certainly won't be." Simple, yet profound. I had to remind myself that losing my hair meant I was doing everything I could to get healthy.

When I showed my son my bald head for the first time, he didn't even flinch. At that moment, I realized the loss of my hair allowed me to gain more insight into who I was as a person and what was truly important in my life.

On May 2, 2011, I had my last chemotherapy treatment. After crossing the chemo finish line, I quickly realized that I had taken only the first step. Just as I went through years of touring as a gymnast, I would go through years of PET scans, CT scans, and blood tests as a cancer survivor. This process wouldn't be nearly as glamorous as the post-Games excitement, but it would become a critical part of my journey, and one I have come to embrace as a positive step toward my goal of remaining healthy.

Cancer has changed me in subtle yet important ways. I am more confident and self-assured than I have ever been in my life. I don't sweat the small stuff. I have learned that it's okay to take a break – there will always be more to do. I have become even more passionate in my work with women's health, childhood obesity, and the sport that gave me the foundation I needed to succeed against all odds. My focus has never been clearer.

The most important lesson I took away from this experience is that life is a precious gift, and we must live and appreciate each day. Cancer, like falling off the balance beam, was a challenge, but it also was a blessing because every bobble, every bump along the way, helped me blaze further down the trail of my life. And hopefully, my trail can serve, even in a small way, as a helping hand for the generations of women who follow behind me.

. . . .

Shannon Miller is the most decorated American gymnast in history and is the only female athlete inducted into the U.S. Olympics Hall of Fame – twice! Her tally of five medals at the 1992 Olympics was the most won by a U.S. athlete. At the 1996 Games, she led the "Magnificent Seven" to the U.S. Women's first ever Team Gold and captured Gold on the Balance Beam for the first time for any American gymnast.

After retiring from Olympic competition, Shannon earned undergraduate degrees in marketing and entrepreneurship and a law degree from Boston College. She then transitioned to analyst and host, appearing on NBC, ABC, Comcast, MSNBC, and others. She is the host of Health and Wellness Channel's The Wish List with Shannon Miller and hosts her weekly radio show, Shannon Miller Lifestyle. Her company, Shannon Miller Lifestyle: Health and Fitness for Women, launched in 2010 with a series of fitness books, DVDs, cookbooks, and the Shannon Miller Walk-Fit program – a free online tracking and incentive program. Shannon is a highly sought-after motivational speaker and advocate for the health and wellness of women and children. As an Olympian, wife, mother, and cancer survivor, Shannon is dedicated to helping women make their health a priority. www.shannonmillerlifestyle.com

Transformational Trailblazing

By Kate Neligan, founder of Mindful Media Entertainment LLC and Synergy TV

I now understand what a "calling" means. In The Blues Brothers, John Belushi and Dan Aykroyd claim they are on a "mission from God." It took me 30 years to see my own divine assignment. Once I found it, however, that awareness completely transformed my life.

My background is in entertainment and digital media. By the age of 31, I had already risen to the position of vice president of a movie studio. Within the course of one year, I had achieved my dream job and doubled my salary. I was so proud of myself, and yet I was deeply unfulfilled. I couldn't understand why. I had manifested everything I thought I wanted, but something was wrong. I felt like I was pretending to be someone I wasn't in an effort to climb the corporate ladder. I knew then that another promotion and more money wasn't going to make me happy.

I was selling horror movies and working in an environment that I felt was full of fear and ruled by power struggles. I knew there had to be another way. I had seen it inside my spiritual communities. I felt a deep sense that the old system, full of competition, greed, fear, and power, was dying. I looked around and saw dinosaurs running businesses, while I was having conversations with my female friends about a better way that we couldn't see yet but knew was coming. I realized then that female entrepreneurs would lead the way into the future. My friends and I were being called to a new system of doing business, a system focused on co-creation, creativity, and synergy. The female way, full of collaboration, support, and mentorship, would help our society thrive again.

It became apparent that to really embrace my mission, I would need to step into my greatness and let go of my old ego ways. I had to find a new way, a new path. I needed to become a trailblazer. All of the resources and qualities I needed to fulfill my mission were within, but I had to unleash them. My layers of hurt, doubt, judgment, and fear were blocking my light, just as the clouds often cover the sun.

I used to sabotage myself a lot. The clouds in my life were the heaviest when I was a teenager and throughout college. I hated who I was, had little self-esteem, and felt like life was hard and pointless. I escaped by drinking, and I quickly found myself in a downward spiral. I ended an amazing relationship with a wonderful man because I didn't think I deserved him. The pain of that breakup forced me to look deeply into the mirror. At 22, I couldn't believe who I had become, and I knew it was time for a change.

Taking responsibility for the life I had created and for the person I had become was not easy at first. I fought against myself. Thankfully, during that time, I was introduced to a book that would profoundly change my life. My mom suggested I read Louise Hay's, "You Can Heal Your Life." At first, I railed and rebelled. I put myself through months of therapy, but I couldn't get out of my own way. Finally, I picked up the book, knowing I had nothing left to lose – and I absorbed it like a sponge. In it, I learned that everyone was doing the best they could with the resources they had available to them. I also learned that I was willing to change. This new awareness and affirmation shifted something inside me, and I began to heal my relationship with myself. That was the tipping point of transformation in my life, as I began my journey of personal development and spirituality.

I have to laugh when I think, "I found God," as I had always judged those words in the past. I was an atheist until I was 23, and I wouldn't even read a book with the word God in it. I harshly judged religion, and science was my bible. If you couldn't prove it to me, it didn't exist. I felt that science explained everything … until it didn't. I started to have so many unbelievable experiences and synchronicities that I just couldn't ignore that there was something larger than me. This realization helped me get out of my head and into my heart, which was the longest, but most important, journey I've ever taken.

I started to realize so many things about myself and the universe through my self-development work. As I attended lectures, took workshops, and studied, I began to spiral upward. I found that I deeply resonated with all of the messages from the various luminaries I was studying, and my definitions of love and God completely changed. I felt called to share the stories with friends, and I realized my transformation was a positive influence and inspiration to others. If I could change from self-hate to self-love, anyone could.

Still, despite my progress, my process of self-awareness and self-compassion had only begun. They say when the student is ready, the teacher appears, and this was the case for me. I was introduced serendipitously to the University of Santa Monica, and I applied to their Master's program in Spiritual Psychology. Two years of deeply profound exercises and skills showed me that miracles happen, people can heal in an instant, and that we are all connected. Not only did I find deep love within myself for the first time, but I started to really love others and, of course, my life. USM became the lighthouse on the shore, which showed me, and others, the way out of our self-induced darkness.

As part of my second year coursework at USM, I was asked to choose a dream project, something that had meaning and heart, something I had always wanted to do. I reflected back on my life and realized my path had been one of transformation and evolution of consciousness. I recognized that I was committed to inspiring others and changing lives. I felt in my heart that I wanted to be of service and leave a legacy. I saw that every step of my journey, especially in my professional career, was leading to one place: to use digital media storytelling to inspire others.

I knew that the uplifting and priceless stories we all have inside needed to be shared. So I began to work 20-hour weeks on my dream of a channel for conscious media on top of my 50-hour weeks at the studio. I wrote a business plan and made a sizzle reel for the first time. I researched and networked, and I started to vision weekly with a friend. They say to do something you have never done you must become someone you have never been. That meant stretching, growing, and learning to be uncomfortable.

My vision grew and became bigger than me. People showed up from unexpected places to offer support and encouragement. I was constantly asked, "How can I help you?" Never before had I seen so much support for anything that I wanted to do. I knew I was on the right track. I knew I was part of the new model of business, and that I could show others how to step into their dreams.

There comes a time when we are all asked to make major life decisions. Trina Paulus asks, "How does one become a butterfly? They must want to fly so much they are willing to give up being a caterpillar." In early 2012, I left corporate America behind to step fully into my role as entrepreneur. I took a leap of faith and risked failing. I left behind the comfortable, the known, the ego-lifestyle, the six-figure salary, and the VP title. I launched my dream of Synergy TV, an inspirational channel for the masses. I began to blaze a new trail for filmmakers, entrepreneurs, advertisers, audiences, and investors to follow.

I intend to show others that we can do well by doing good. I believe we can create successful business models where it's safe for women to be feminine, and where we can support each other from our authentic selves. I know we can save the world by saving ourselves first and getting out of our own way. It is time for us to synergize the practical and the spiritual, the business world and the divine world. My dream is to create a new economic and studio paradigm that is based on synergy, connections, and collaboration. My intention is to transform lives for the better, through entertainment, enlightenment, and inspiration.

. . . .

Kate Neligan is founder and CEO of Mindful Media Entertainment LLC, a conscious media studio poised to elevate the collective consciousness of the planet through mindful movies and transformational television. MME is the parent company of Synergy TV, an on demand and online channel that entertains, enlightens, and inspires. Formerly, Kate was vice president of on demand and digital marketing at Lionsgate, where she launched and promoted the digital sales and distribution group's large slate of new release and catalog movies and television shows. Kate handled all marketing campaigns, media buying, and partner relationships for the studio's video on demand and digital download business. She is most proud of the charity promotions she conceptualized and executed, including an "Inner PRECIOUSness" cable tour with Dress for Success and Women In Cable Telecommunications.

Previously, Kate was marketing manager at the American Film Institute's Digital Content Lab, where she handled marketing, publicity, and event planning. Before AFI, Kate worked at iN Demand, where she built relationships with VOD/PPV sales representatives, cable systems, and studios while being the point person for Video On Demand during the product's initial launch. Kate is a graduate of Lafayette College in Pennsylvania and the University of Santa Monica, where she earned her Master's degree in Spiritual Psychology. www.synergytvnetwork.com

I am a Trailblazer.

1. I step fully into my life purpose and into my personal power.

2. I visualize my goals and create actionable steps to help me reach them.

3. I am brave with each small step and each large leap – even in my thoughts, where my magnificence begins.

4. I create my own example.

5. I act to honor and support those ahead of me, those alongside me, and those behind me.

wisdom

Anne Frank

"Riches, prestige, everything can be lost. But the happiness in your own heart can only be dimmed; it will always be there, as long as you live, to make you happy again." – Anne Frank, February 23, 1944

Through her poignant words, young Anne Frank demonstrated that feminine wisdom can exist independent of age.

. . . .

Anne Frank is known across the world for her earnest, heartfelt, and heartbreaking journal, "The Diary of a Young Girl," also known as "Diary of Anne Frank." Written between June 12, 1942, and August 1, 1944, the diary chronicles Anne's life during WWII. Though she was born in Frankfurt, Anne fled to Amsterdam with her Jewish family in 1933, shortly after Hitler's Nazi Party rose to power. Less than a month after her 13th birthday, the Nazis invaded the Netherlands, and Anne and her family went into hiding in a secret, three-room annex located in the attic of her father's office. It was there that Anne wrote the vast majority of the diary's entries.

As a young girl, Anne's dream was to become a journalist, "to have something besides a husband and children" to which she could devote herself. So, she turned to her diary. Within its pages, she expressed with startling insight her fear, her boredom, her hope, and her aspirations.

Unfortunately, Anne's dreams of growing up were not meant to be. An unidentified informer notified the German Security Police of the family's hidden location on August 4, 1944. The police stormed the annex and arrested the Frank family. Anne, her sister Margot, and her mother were sent to the Auschwitz concentration camp. In March 1945, after being transferred to Bergen-Belsen, Anne and Margot died of typhus.

Despite her shortened life, Anne accomplished one of her life's primary goals through her diary. "I want to be useful or bring enjoyment to all people, even those I've never met," she wrote. "I want to go on living even after my death!" Indeed, she has.

Her diary has been praised the world over for its sophisticated writing style, its honesty, and its wisdom. Even in hiding, Anne's faith in humankind couldn't be shaken. "Despite everything, I believe that people are really good at heart," she wrote.

Since the diary's initial publication in 1950, a Pulitzer Prize-winning play has been based on it, as well as a successful movie. Classrooms all across the United States regularly read Anne's diary as part of the standard curriculum. In the words of Eleanor Roosevelt, Anne's diary is "one of the wisest and most moving commentaries on war and its impact on human beings" ever written.

• •

• Spent just over two years in hiding to escape the Nazis, 1942-1944

• Author of one of the world's most widely read books

Eleanor Roosevelt

"Life must be lived and curiosity kept alive. One must never, for whatever reason, turn his back on life." – Eleanor Roosevelt

Eleanor Roosevelt reshaped the world's perception of women with her unwavering wisdom, optimism, charm, and humility.

. . . .

Anna Eleanor Roosevelt was born on October 11, 1884, in New York City. The niece of President Theodore Roosevelt, she was an automatic member of wealthy high society. Despite this privileged background, Eleanor met tragedy early through the successive deaths of her mother, her father, and one of her brothers. Raised by her grandmother from early adolescence, Eleanor was left feeling hungry for affection and wishing for physical beauty. By 14, she had realized a pretty face was not necessary to create and attract good character. "No matter how plain a woman may be," she wrote, "if truth and loyalty are stamped upon her face, all will be attracted to her."

At 15, Eleanor began school at the Allenswood Academy in London. There, she learned to speak French and gained the glowing self-confidence that would radiate from her for the rest of her life. In 1905, she married her distant cousin, Franklin D. Roosevelt. President Roosevelt gave her away.

In 1921, after Franklin became paralyzed by a disease everyone believed to be polio, Eleanor started to accompany him on public appearances. Sometimes she even appeared in his stead. After Franklin was elected governor of New York, Eleanor's involvement in New York Democratic politics escalated sharply. She campaigned for women's suffrage, rights in the work place, a 48-hour work week, a guaranteed minimum wage, and the instatement of child labor laws.

In 1933, Franklin was elected President of the United States, and Eleanor became one of the first activist First Ladies. She wrote a regular column and held more than 300 press conferences to educate the public about White House policies and her work with the New Deal, the establishment of the National Youth Administration, the budding civil rights movement and NAACP, and women's rights. When World War II broke out, Eleanor dedicated her work to the war effort by supporting civilian volunteerism and visiting U.S. troops overseas.

After Franklin's death in 1945, Eleanor became a delegate to the United

Nations General Assembly. As Chairperson for the Commission of Human Rights, she considered herself an ambassador for the common man and woman and represented humanitarian, cultural, and social issues. Fellow delegates revered Eleanor for her common sense, optimism, humor, energy, and charm.

In 1948, Eleanor penned the original draft of the Universal Declaration of Human Rights, which affirmed equal rights to life and liberty for all people. "We wanted as many nations as possible to accept the fact that men, for one reason or another, were born free and equal in dignity and rights, that they were endowed with reason and conscience, and should act toward one another in a spirit of brotherhood," she wrote.

Eleanor also was a key player in the establishment of Israel, and she negotiated with the Soviet Union after World War II. She published several books about her life and died, at 78 years old, on November 7, 1962, in New York City. She is famously remembered by Democratic presidential candidate, Adlai Stevenson, as someone who "would rather light a candle than curse the darkness."

. . . .

• Drafted the Universal Declaration of Human Rights

• Served as both the First Lady of New York and the First Lady of the United States

• Promoted equal rights for all races, genders, and religions

• Elected Chairperson of the United Nations Commission of Human Rights

 # Essays By Women

Living the Feminine Power

By Jenny Craig, LCSW, BCD, author of the books "I am Brilliant," "Weighing your Options," and "Live your Power - Battling your inner bully," and founder of the Live your Power program.

. . . .

One evening, while I was enjoying a relaxing dinner, I began to get countless calls and texts. I excused myself from the table to discover that a woman I knew was on a mission to destroy my character and reputation. As I returned my missed calls and read my e-mails, I discovered she had sent malicious misinformation about me to newspapers, magazines, and local media stations. I felt like I was in a made-for-television movie!

I contacted an attorney who advised me to call the police. It was then that I came across a quote from Eleanor Roosevelt that read, "You gain strength, courage, and confidence by every experience in which you really stop to look fear in the face." It was the message I needed to hear. I decided to reach deep within myself to find my own strength and confidence – and what I discovered surprised me.

Though I was a licensed therapist, whose purpose was to help people find their inner power and live it on a daily basis, I realized I was not being completely authentic in living my own power. I had resisted taking care of myself first, and I had allowed negative thoughts and patterns to suck away my energy. In fact, I had allowed myself to be bullied by a force much stronger than the woman I had so feared – my own inner bully. That powerful, nasty voice had allowed the woman into my life because of my own thoughts of being unlovable and unworthy!

Once I recognized I needed to bring light to the darkness my inner bully had allowed into my life, I set out to cleanse my life of negativity. I gathered together numerous tools from neurology, psychology, and spirituality, and my experiences of being a clinical therapist to strengthen my voice of inner power. As I learned to be vulnerable and compassionate with myself, I also opened up more inspiration within myself, inspiration that allowed me to create additional tools to help us all live the life of joy we deserve.

One day, as I moved ahead in my journey, I woke up in a blissful state and jotted down, "Today I woke up, and I was everything I wanted to be. I forgave myself for everything, as I finally realized I was just learning from the experience. I allowed myself to love everyone everywhere … even those who hurt me." I then set the intention to empower all those who crossed my path.

Here is what I learned on my journey to discover and live my own power:

Forgiveness is a powerful tool we can use to reconnect to our inner power. Research shows that the chemicals released within the body when we forgive help lift depression, calm anxiety, and stop headaches, backaches, stomachaches, and more. Further, when we remain angry and/or hurt, the chemicals and hormones we release can make us sick. As Nelson Mandela once said, "Resentment is like drinking poison and waiting for it to kill your enemy."

On my journey of gratefulness, I was unable to forgive the people who hurt me until I learned the true definition of forgiveness, which is to let go or untie the person or experience that caused us harm. Staying resentful of someone only gives that person the power to hold us back from being our greatest selves. Releasing the resentment sets us free to be who we are. Catherine Ponder states, "When you hold resentment toward another, you are bound to that person or condition by an emotional link that is stronger than steel. Forgiveness is the only way to dissolve that link and get free." This realization enabled me to release the people, experiences, and residual emotions I had built up and to allow space for my healing.

Focus on the positive people in your life. Every 60 seconds of worrying steals one minute of joy. Think back to the people who helped you during your difficult experience. Allow yourself to experience their kindness and unselfishness, and share your gratitude with them. My unpleasant situation enabled me to see just how much love and support I received from friends, family, and acquaintances. I chose to focus on the outpouring of support, instead of worrying about the negative things being said about me.

Make your own joy a priority. Just as we are taught on an airplane to place an air source on ourselves first, we also need to fill with internal joy before we can give to others. Healthy giving includes the assumption that we are giving from the abundance in our lives. When others tap into our joy tank and siphon away our energy, it is not a healthy relationship. Through my experience, I realized that my relationship with the bully had never been a healthy one; I had felt drained after each of our encounters. This experience taught me to value my joy and to ensure that there is even energy flow in all of my relationships.

Listen to your female intuition. Each time I have met a bully in my life, I have had a gut instinct that told me to stay away or I may get hurt. As I reflected on my life, it became clear to me that I had a pattern of ignoring my gut in favor of choosing to believe that everyone had good intentions in mind. I discovered that I was being self-centered in my belief that everyone's perception of the world was the same as my own.

Be grateful. Just 20 seconds after we think a grateful thought, our brains and bodies are flooded with chemicals associated with gratefulness. These chemicals help us feel better. Allow yourself five minutes in the morning and five minutes before bed to think grateful thoughts.

Appreciate your own self-development. When I first learned of the lies the woman had spread about me, I was devastated. It took me some time to realize that my devastation was less about what she said than it was about my inner bully's nasty insinuations that she was right. When I realized my feelings were the result of my own inner negativity, I decided not to allow my obstacles to be significant enough to disable or destroy me. Instead, I decided I would take them for what they were – opportunities for growth – and learn from them. Every experience we have provides us with an opportunity to grow and learn, to become better, to become more whole. Uncover the lesson from your own experiences, and be grateful for the good things they have brought into your life.

Who knew that such a seemingly devastating event could help me release my vulnerability, compassion, and female intuition? Ironically, it was through the ongoing negative attacks that I made quantum leaps in my soul's development. While I was horrified that I had to spend time defending all I had accomplished, I also was gifted with the opportunity to become a newer, stronger woman. Each and every time the bully made an untrue claim, I was offered the gift to look within, where I discovered a unique, brilliant inner power that is my place of absolute peace, inspiration, and divine connection.

As I began to feed my voice of inner power on a daily basis, I watched my life change. The negative people and experiences left my life, which created space for more positive ones to enter. It was then that I realized it is those vulnerable enough to reveal their challenges that help change the world. It is from shedding light onto our pain that we can reclaim our inner power. From this place of authenticity, we can stand up for what we believe to be right and encourage others to do so, also.

As I began to love myself more, others began to ask me how they could do the same. From living my own power, I found myself gifted with the opportunity to help others grow and change. Since then, I have written a guide and created a simple yet extremely powerful program to share the tools I used to heal. The Live your Power program teaches how to clear out emotional residue, clear out energy vampires, create boundaries, train the brain for positivity, and live a life of joy. As these tools are not often taught in traditional schooling, I also encourage people to share the tools with others.

In addition to the Live your Power program, I was blessed to become part of the grateful ring movement in which people share their inner gratitude with those who have brought light into their worlds. I have found gratitude from my experience, and it has spread farther than I can imagine. As Buddha once said, "Thousands of candles can be lit from a single candle." May we always allow the light within us to brighten the world around us.

. . . .

Jenny Craig, LCSW, BCD has a background in neurology and psychology and has studied in nine different countries. An international coach at Insite Strategist and the creator of the Live your Power™ program, Jenny also hosts the Live your Power hour, writes the Ask Jenny column, and is a sought-after keynote speaker, providing professional training seminars in 48 states. Author of "Weighing Your Options;" "Live your Power - Tools to battle your inner bully;" and "I am Brilliant," a children's book on inner beauty and brilliance, she also is one of the contributors to the bestselling book, "Living upside down, Thinking right side up," and has been published in numerous magazines. As creator of the "I am grateful for...™" ring, Jenny was featured on a PBS Brain Power video and spoke at the Energy of Success Summit and the Designing a Powerful Woman Summit. She also has recorded CDs for professionals, including "Bully proofing your clients," "101 Quick Techniques to help children with emotional and behavioral problems," and "Emotional Eating: Strategies for Lifelong Changes." Always giving back, she is the 2011-2012 vice president of the American Women's Business Association and district chair for youth services for the International Kiwanis Organization. www.liveyourpower.com

Three Gifts from My Grandmother

By Sally Franz, author of the Amazon Bestseller "Scrambled Leggs"

....

What would stop you from having joy in your life? Suddenly being paralyzed from the chest down? Having your heart broken by the discovery that your husband is cheating on you? Your mother's death? The death of a good friend? A cancer scare? Losing your home? Moving away from all of your friends? Suffering chronic, daily pain for the rest of your life?

What if all of that happened in one year?

That was my life a few years back. All at once, life's miseries came rushing forward, like water behind a weak dam. One day, whoosh, it broke loose. Suddenly, life's everyday annoyances – traffic jams, kids with attitude, an ungrateful spouse – seemed like a walk in the park.

Any woman who has had the rug pulled out from under her understands feeling completely helpless, while still being the one who is supposed to be in control. As women, we are culturally looked upon as the center of the home and the family. When life beats us down, we may wonder what kind of cruel joke fate is playing. "How can I hold the family together, Lord," we might ask, "if I have no strength, resources, or help?"

That year, within a span of 30 minutes, I became paralyzed. At the time, I was the youth director at a large church, and I was skiing with about 20 high school kids. Out of nowhere, I felt a strange tingling start in my left big toe and travel up my leg. Within moments, it had numbed my entire leg, and I fell. I managed to get to a base lodge in time for the paralysis to make it up the other leg and head for my heart. I frantically searched for an emergency phone number card to call another chaperone on the trip. But, guess what? No card. I was the main caregiver and a mom. Everyone knows moms are supposed to take care of everyone else – we aren't allowed to get sick! A backup chaperone hadn't even been on the radar.

As I was taken away in the ambulance, everything I had planned for, worked for, was sure God had wanted for me dissolved. I had contracted Transverse Myelitis. Like Multiple Sclerosis, it can flow between devastating attacks and remission. Though I am in remission now, I still have pain, neuropathy, energy depletion, complications with digestion, and more. But, I can walk. (Well, sort of, if staggering counts.) And, that is a vast improvement.

When my first attack hit, it was as if everything I had counted on as real or lasting evaporated: my health, my husband, my home. It wasn't a matter of picking up the pieces; there were no pieces left. All I had was a huge question mark over my head, as in "What just happened here?"

Then something strange happened. Out of my medicated stupor materialized three wise feminine traits my Grandmother taught me: faith, curiosity, and humor.

My grandmother was the queen of "teaching moments." One of her hobbies was raising butterflies. As a child, I often helped her feed the caterpillars. I would watch the chrysalis for what seemed like months, and then, finally, one day a lovely butterfly would emerge. "When you can't see what's going on in the chrysalis, you just have to have faith that a miracle is forming," my grandmother would say.

Faith, unfortunately, is best learned when we feel hopeless. Like patience, I never pray for it. I know what's going to show up next – a need for it! But, life has a way of testing us, no matter how well we control our day-to-day lives. With faith, hidden strengths turn up when we need them, seemingly from thin air.

The courage and stamina I felt during my first recovery were unlike anything I had felt before. Though I had to fall face-first many times before I could walk, I walked. Though I had to work four to six hours a day on my rehab exercises, I persevered. My faith assured me I would walk again; it gave me strength.

My grandmother used to say, "Women are stronger than they appear. Look at the daffodil. It looks delicate and frilly. But it can bend under a gale force wind, bounce upright, and remain unflustered. Bruised but not broken, because it is rooted down deep in something solid."

That something solid is faith.

Curiosity was another value my grandmother taught me. I used to call her, "Grand-Mother Nature;" she was curious about everything. One day, when I was about five, she befriended a lime green garter snake. I was terrified at the sight of it slithering all around her arm.

"Don't be afraid of the snake," she told me. "It's much more afraid of you. Do you know how it smells? From the end of its tongue. Isn't that silly? What if your nose was on the end of your tongue?"

Then, she laughed and held up her new friend. Gently, she placed him in my arms, and I wiggled as it slithered. "He's here to eat the bugs that attack my flowers so I am glad to have found him," she said and smiled.

I still can't bring myself to pick up a strange snake, but I remember that day's vital lesson. Through curiosity, we can observe and investigate a situation without judgment. We can remove ourselves from the situation long enough to learn compassion for others and see our way to reconciliation.

Curiosity enables me to stop the "Monster Lies" in my head. "Why me?" or "Whose fault is it?" keeps me in the past. "What's next?" moves me forward. A better question from a curious mind becomes, "Where could this lead me?" "Given what I have now, what can I do?" "What can I do now that I couldn't do before?" Wiser questions achieve wiser results. Curiosity saves me from self-pity and discouragement. It makes me wise.

I used to tell my children, if you read a sad story and it seems as though the king and queen and their children died in a fire and the castle is in ashes, don't close the book and cry. Get curious. Flip the page to the next chapter. You'll likely find they all escaped through a secret passageway and are safe and sound. Keep reading, the happy ending will be there.

My grandmother also gifted me with a sense of humor. Through laughter, humor transforms us from victim to victor. Laughter releases endorphins that make us feel good and give us hope. From my grandmother, I learned how to see the funny side of the downside. If dinner got burned, she laughed. We all laughed. If milk got spilt, we laughed. (Of course, we still had to clean it up!) I learned to use humor to fight bullies, to win approval, and to calm a conflict. When people were sick, dying, and scared, we used humor to draw closer together as a family. We told stories and jokes, and we watched comedy on TV.

When I found myself in a wheelchair, facing a year of therapy just to walk again and a life that was spinning out of control, I used these three wise gifts from the woman I loved. She taught me that to be a woman meant to have the strength and the wisdom to face life head-on and to lovingly embrace its challenges and sorrows. Life wasn't necessarily going to be easy, but it was only going to be as hard as I chose to make it.

In faith, I clung to the knowledge that I was not alone and that a miracle was secretly growing inside me, which would be revealed in due time. Faith was not so much an effort as a choice. Choosing to wait for a miracle to present itself became exciting, not grueling. What magical butterfly would appear this time?

As I began to try to find a purpose to this new altered state, or what the military calls "the new normal," I had to ask, what was God up to now? I felt like Private Benjamin. True, I didn't like the colors of the uniforms or my schedule, but rather than resist the program and end up marching in circles in the rain, I decided it was time to discover my new mission.

I began to look for clues every day. As my curiosity grew, I became more willing to give up my expectations of what the new adventure would look like. I still had goals, but I wasn't married to how I achieved them anymore. Being curious about my life was like sitting in the grass with my grandmother learning about nature as it revealed itself. Slowly my life revealed new opportunities, like the opportunity to help other women with T.M. in a Facebook support group. Our group has only two requirements: You have to have T.M., and you have to have a sense of humor.

As I learned from my grandmother so long ago, humor is a tool for transformation and nurturing. It also is a key to feminine power. It also is just plain fun! I laugh at my humanity and at my circumstances, and I encourage others to laugh even when not-so-funny things happen (such as getting paralyzed.) Yes, there is a time for somber compassion, but there also is time for joy that spills over into non-stop giggle fits, the kind that make us laugh so hard we cry.

Because of the feminine wisdom I have gained, I have managed to bounce back from gale force winds, even as they continue pounding. My strength sustains me. Some days, it is all I can do to hang on until the next day. But, as a dear woman friend reminded me, peace comes when we don't need life to be predictable. It is enough that we have faith in a reliable God. Once I gave up having to know the outcome of all of this, it was much easier to laugh and have fun in the moment.

Let me end with this wonderful story. After I was released from the physical rehabilitation center, several of my women friends piled me into a van and took me on a road trip from California to Las Vegas. The popular ad campaign that year was, "What Happens in Vegas, Stays in Vegas." We were all over 50 so our trip slogan was, "What Falls Off in Vegas, Stays in Vegas."

We went to shows, drove through the Red Rocks, ate lots of chocolate, and went out to dinner. It was a marvelous time, a time for laughter and for healing. As women, our wise souls innately knew how to laugh, how to commiserate, and how to love in ways that filled the hollows of my broken heart. It was through the other women that I was able to rediscover and amplify my own strength. And, it is from this wonderfully secure place of inner strength that I am able to move forward into the great unknown of my life, as my chrysalis turns into a butterfly.

. . . .

Sally Franz has been a motivational speaker, a stand-up comic in NYC, and a TV and radio personality. She has appeared on national television on the Maury Povich Show, CNBC Lifestyles, and three times on The Today Show. Additionally, she is a corporate trainer with clients such as Intel, SONY, Texaco-Chevron, Yahoo!, The City of New York, and The City of Los Angeles. She is a ghostwriter and book doctor and has written eight books of her own. One of her stories was included in The New York Times Bestselling Series, "Chicken Soup for the Soul." Her most recent book, an Amazon Bestseller, is "Scrambled Leggs ... A Snarky Tale of Hospital Hooey." For more information, visit www.SallyFranz.com.

How to Do This Thing We Call Life

Lessons my mother taught me ...

By Sue Lee, author of "Whispers of Color for Adults" and "Whispers of Color for Children," and creator of "I Believe in Me!"

. . . .

We come into this life as innocent children, full of awe and wonder, clinging to the women we come to know as "Mom," "Mother," "Provider," and "Friend." From birth, we watch and mimic these women who delivered us out of the hope that they also will teach us "how to be" in this world, how to not only survive, but to thrive. As women, our heritage is one of sharing. This heritage becomes a thread that carries over the generations and gets passed along – woman to woman, mother to daughter. It is a thread that weaves a feminine tapestry we women come to depend upon and recognize as our feminine fabric.

My mother was the most amazing woman I have ever had the privilege to know, and I admired her from the first memory I have of her to the last one. Everything about her reinforced her ability to "teach" with grace. She was light, love, enthusiasm, and determination. But, this is not just my story; this is our feminine story, the universal bonding of mother and daughter that becomes one melding and can never be destroyed.

I'm the youngest of three children and the only girl. My siblings and I grew up on a little farm, in a deciduous forest with a driveway that seemed miles long to a little girl's legs but actually was some three hundred feet. Ours was a challenged life in some ways, poor enough to qualify for welfare, yet stubborn enough not to accept it. Our house began as a small cottage without a bathroom and would remain so for the first twelve years of my life.

We were mostly dependent upon our garden and the animals we reared for food. In many ways, we lived an idyllic life because my mother made it so. Her name was Rose, and like her namesake's flower, she stood out with her own characteristics and fragrance for living. She believed negative thoughts were exactly what they implied – negative – so why wallow in them, when you could linger with the good that was right there every day before your eyes, from dawn to dusk to dawn again. Why wallow when the next day's reawakening life was there to be discovered and enjoyed?

From the time I was very small, my mother worked to teach me how to do this thing we call life – how to embody the feminine traits of strength and perspective with the eyes of the heart, and how not to focus on the disempowering, the ugly, the disheartening. We didn't have a bathroom, though everyone else did, and our dishtowels were made from old cloth sacks. Brightly colored rag rugs covered our worn linoleum instead of the Persian carpets that others used. Yet, amongst this poverty, my life sparkled with joy, laughter, and cleanliness. Early on, my mother taught me to view anything I owned as a gift. "Come to know it for what it is, treasure it, and treat it with value," she said.

What we had, we appreciated, and it showed in the way we lived. Our animals were treated with respect, and we gave grace for our food and for the lives that provided us with needed nourishment. Like the animals, our garden was highly valued, and I spent hours and hours next to my mother, weeding our way down rows of vegetables.

When you work side by side, tending for that which will feed you, you come to really know the person beside you. Conversations merge through the seasons, the harvest, and the canning. My mother and I were blessed, as were women long ago, to spend hours in the company of other female voices. Other mothers came to our fields with their daughters, and we'd all laugh and talk as we stored food for our future use. Our friendships ran deep, and I am grateful to this day for the hours spent amongst all those shared hearts.

Mom's wisdom seemed limitless. She taught life lessons in a way my friends envied, for she magically delivered insights in the simplest of forms. When I was just five, she taught me the power of lasting love. One day, I asked my mother to watch as I made a peanut butter and jelly sandwich. "Will you watch me make a sandwich?" I asked in my little-girl way.

"Look, I put the peanut butter on just like you," I said as I spread the sticky substance on the bread. "Look, I put the jelly on just like you."

She nodded and smiled that knowing smile of hers, the smile that communicated she knew exactly where this encounter would lead.

"Look, I put the pieces together, just like you. I cut it corner to corner to make triangles, just like you. Now, watch Mom . . . I'm going to bite it and chew."

I took my first bite, chewed quickly, and swallowed. Something was wrong, "How come yours taste better?" I asked.

With a twinkle in her eye, she replied, "Well, Sues, I believe the feeling we have when we do a thing stays with us, no matter what we do, whether we're cleaning house, caring for the garden, cooking, talking to others, or just living life. There's an energy there, and someday when you've grown up, I bet some scientist will prove it. But, really I don't care if it is ever proven because I believe it to be true. So when no one is looking, I throw in a dash of love. I prefer to cook that way because I believe it can be tasted, and see? You just confirmed it."

I never forgot that lesson, delivered so simply that even a five-year-old could learn it through just one example.

My life overflowed with similar lessons, lessons taught by my mom, lessons that women instinctively have known and have passed down since the beginning of time. One day when I was eight, I came home from school with the knowledge that I had called my brother a name in front of other children still heavy in my mind.

After dinner, Mom said, "Sues, I'd like to talk with you a second." She walked with me to the sofa. "I understand you called your brother a name today," she said.

I nodded, but said nothing. She proceeded. "I don't care what you think of your brother or what you call your brother, but I do care what you think of my son and what you call my son . . . he's my son . . . I love him." By that time I was already crying, but she calmly continued. "I love my son, as I love you, and I wouldn't want anyone to think badly of my daughter or call her a name. I will always love you and support you. I know you didn't mean to hurt him or to hurt me. I want you to understand that when you call someone a name, you hurt others, and I know you don't want to be known as someone who does that."

So simple, so well-expressed. She delivered feminine ethics packaged in the daily living of life, and taught me a perspective that I could instantly take in and make my own.

We were poor, but that didn't keep us from attending what Mom called the free institution of life's lessons – the mall. Every so often, Mom would say, "Let's go to the mall." We weren't going to shop, and I knew it. We'd have a quarter to share. She'd buy a coffee. I'd buy a root beer. And, we'd sit there and watch.

"Look around," she'd say. "Who do you think is happy? Kind? Smart? Angry? Sad? Intelligent?"

I'd pick people I'd see and say, "That woman there, she might be sad."

"Why do you think that?" Mom would ask.

I'd describe how the lady stood, walked, and acted. On and on it would go . . . then came the insight.

"Sue, you can be anything you wish to be and become like anyone you wish to become. Just 'be' it, become the trait you wish to have. If you want confidence, walk like you have it. If you want to be interested, walk like you're interested, and act like you're interested in that which is around you. If you don't know how to do something, watch others . . . see what they do. If it's a trait you wish to emulate, then do so."

That feminine survival skill of awareness, of noticing and becoming, has served me well throughout my life, particularly when I became a foreign exchange student at the age of seventeen. I never faltered during that time; I watched, observed, and used all the skills and knowledge my mother had already shared with me. Joyfully, I went about England, with the knowledge that my mom was with me, that her thoughts and lessons guided me as I represented the best of who I was and was still to become.

As the years passed, my mother's wisdom only grew. She shared and shared, and I continued to take it in. I used the lessons my mother taught me throughout the years: first, when I received a full grant to attend college; then, years later, when I found myself behind the Berlin Wall in what was then East Germany as an adult representative for our church.

I am my mother's daughter. I have a zest for life that is unstoppable. I get up before the sun to welcome each day and linger with God. Like my mother, I believe my life is my prayer, that how I speak, walk, and listen is my direct communication for all that I have and all for which I'm grateful.

I'm fortunate as an adult to have numerous female friends. As a group, we conscientiously explore this journey of life. Like women who gathered at the river so long ago, we come together to learn, to know, and to share. We laugh, we cry, we remember. We enhance our perspective of life through activities and discussion, and we are fully aware that we have chosen to pass our feminine knowledge along. We are remembering our womanly heritage and are claiming it . . . we the modern women of cell phones, computers, and websites. And, every time we meet, I think of my mom, who would have so loved such community. After all, I learned it from her and from those women and girls we worked with side by side, so long ago on our little farm.

The little girl I once was – that barefoot, carefree, enthusiastic, motivated child – learned to believe in herself, to know she could become *anything* her heart desired. Through my mother's lessons, I learned I could become the heroine of my own life's story, and I have. The little girl who grew up wearing her brother's hand-me-down clothes, who didn't have a bathroom until she was twelve, that little girl, now a mom and a grandmother herself, put the lessons her mother taught her into a twice-nationally recognized DVD for preschoolers. It's called, "I Believe in Me!" and rightly so.

I have gone from rags to recognition because of my mom's lessons. And, like the women before me, I've chosen to pass along what I've learned. Those valued lessons now rest within a program for children, children whom I will never know but who will now hear, "Give it a try, and soon, you'll say, 'I did it!'" I am my mother's daughter, a woman sharing her wisdom of how to do this thing we call life.

. . . .

Sue Lee is a Life Management Skills educator and the creator of "I Believe in Me!" a DVD for preschoolers, which received two national recognitions – a Parents' Choice Award and a KIDS FIRST! media endorsement. She also is the author of two books of poetry: "Whispers of Color for Adults" and "Whispers of Color for Children." Her speaking engagements have included the National Forum on Character Education and the Eunice Kennedy Shriver Community of Caring Conference, Beyond Bullying. Sue is available for presentations at conferences, schools, and retreats to address the importance of positive emotional intelligence, becoming the hero or heroine in your own life's story, and developing character and confidence instead of trying to "turn around" a troubled teen. Sue also wrote the first chapter of her husband

William H. Lee M.D.'s new book, "Over 50 Feeling 30." www.ibelieveinme.tv

ℒiving Wisdom

By Kathryn Peters-Brinkley, author of "Jewels for the Soul: Spiritual Reflections and Affirmations for the Heart and Soul," and publisher of the acclaimed online publication, Kinetics Magazine: Awakening to Ascension.

....

As a journalist, what I have always enjoyed most is the *art of the interview*. For over 20 years, I have thrilled at the prospect and jumped at the chance to indulge in deliciously meaningful conversation with someone deemed, by the world, truly wise. From Marianne Williamson to Wayne Dyer, and Louise Hay to Michael Beckwith, I have interviewed the gamut of the most prominent leaders in the New Thought and spiritual arena. Indeed, all of them left me deeply moved by the breadth of their profound passion and sweeping insight, on every subject imaginable. Each interview forever changed me. Yet, with nearly 150 such interviews under my belt, I can honestly say that my grandmother, Dora, remains the wisest woman I've ever met. I always called her, "Mama."

As a little girl, I spent a lot of time with Mama because we shared a bedroom. She came to live with us when I was about five years old; she was just over sixty. She'd raised six children, and never worked outside the home. Yet, her mind was razor sharp and eternally curious. Each morning, Mama devoured the newspaper as soon as it was delivered. Each evening, she dutifully sat in the same chair to absorb the evening news with Walter Cronkite. Mama's interest in current world events was insatiable. Whenever possible, I would sit beside her while Cronkite delivered his authoritative rendering of the day's happenings.

While I enjoyed the news itself, I always found Mama's reaction to the commentary far more fascinating. It tickled me to sit at her side and study her responses. She had very strong opinions and excellent judgment. Long before I knew what it meant, I was practicing goddess worship. As a child, I often thought the world would be a better, more peaceful, loving place if everyone would just listen to my Mama!

Her strong opinions were not restricted to local, state, national, and international politics. Oh, no – Mama was a full-spectrum thinker! From sunup to sundown, she shared pearls of wisdom on a myriad of subjects. I guess you could say that Mama was the family therapist and resident sage. My entire family turned to her for love, advice, comfort, and counsel. We marveled at her grasp of reality, the easeful way she dealt with challenges, and her practical application of grounded common sense, in any given situation.

Nothing ever flustered Mama. For my family, she was the anchor that kept us all securely fastened to one another, in love and respect, even in the midst of life's worst storms. Mama's boundless wisdom was built on her three basic concepts: *Family first* (and the whole world is your family;) *Always do your best* (or don't bother to do it at all;) and *Be of good cheer* (no matter the circumstances.) She believed that if you implemented these three straightforward perspectives into your daily endeavors, you simply couldn't go wrong.

Seven days a week, Mama took care of her immediate family first and then looked for others in her extended family – the neighborhood – to help. She babysat for busy moms and went grocery shopping for sick friends. Mama's philosophy was simple: life is a community affair. We are all in this together, and when we take it upon ourselves to be there for one another, we make life better for everyone.

Mama was an absolute stickler on doing things the right way, the first time. She would never suffer a task, no matter how large or small, completed in a shoddy fashion. "If a job is worth doing," she would say, "it is worth doing well." She was a living example of this; she put her heart and soul into every pie she made, every room she cleaned, everyone she loved. Mama trained me to have pride in myself and in all of the things I endeavored to achieve. She didn't believe in cutting corners or making excuses for sloppy work. By always doing our very best, Mama knew, we would have nothing to make excuses for and increased self-esteem, to boot.

No matter what life delivered to her front door each day, Mama was determined to be of good cheer. She considered birth, death, and everything going on in-between holy aspects of our divine journey, with each of them taking their turn to ride on the grand wheel of life. Mama felt to be cheerful in the face of challenge was the best way to turn that miserable challenge into a joyful opportunity. Never did she succumb to gloominess or depression. She stepped up, with courage and optimism, to the bleakest of circumstances. Her faith in God and her own ability to persevere were unshakable. She started each morning with a little bit of red lipstick and her best smile, which overflowed with good cheer!

Another cornerstone of Mama's wisdom was the belief that the quality of our lives is predicated on the strength of our relationships. Paramount for

Mama was her relationship to God. Carving out time and a place of solitude to commune regularly with God was of the utmost importance. Mama never attended a church, nor subscribed to a particular organized religion, but she undertook with joy all of the daily chores she routinely attended, in service to God. With that attitude firmly planted in her heart, the most mundane tasks attained sacred status. Because of her precious relationship with God, when Mama prepared a meal for our family, did the weekly laundry, or helped one of us get over a heartache, she performed independent and collective holy acts of love.

Mama also believed in nurturing her relationship with herself. She was born under the astrological sign of Capricorn, which made her, by nature, quite disciplined and organized. She created a daily regime of wellness, from which she very rarely diverted. She got up and went to bed at the same time every day. She carried out her private prayer ritual before she drank her morning coffee and read the newspaper. She ate breakfast and performed her housecleaning in time to watch her "stories" on television. Her day went on like this, in compartments of allotted time, until she went to bed at night. Only an atomic bomb could have made Mama deviate from her personal schedule. This schedule made her feel secure and self-nurtured, with firm boundaries and clear goals. This is how she loved herself best. This is how she knew she was being trustworthy with her own needs and values. This is how she taught me to do the same.

Because Mama felt we were meant to dance unencumbered in the flow of life, she encouraged me to create a quality of harmony in my relationships with others. Mama would say that on the wings of harmony, anything that disturbed the flow of life could be lifted to an elevated space – the space where ultimate resolution resides. It wasn't that she didn't acknowledge the reality of inevitable disagreements and disputes; she just believed the spiritual undercurrent of any disparity ultimately led to mutual growth. With that in mind, she consistently taught me to look for the lesson being offered, instead of dwelling on being upset over the disagreement. To this day, I hold dear Mama's sagacious advice; I'm always conscious of discerning the gift at the core of every challenge I encounter along my way. It keeps me ever alert, in the now, and fully present to embrace life's intrinsic mystery and magic!

When Mama transitioned, in the summer of 1979, I was pregnant with my second child. I remember getting the dreaded call in the middle of the night. The next morning, I stepped outside into the sunshiny warmth of the day with an emotion akin to resentment. How could the sun be shining, and the birds singing, when Mama was gone? I was furious ... something in the world should be different because I would never be the same! My Mama and all of her wisdom were no longer here with me. How would anything ever feel normal or right again?

That discombobulating state of mind gradually diminished over time, and a few months before the birth of my second daughter, I had a dream. In that dream, Mama sat with me on the swing in my backyard. She held my hand ever so gently, looked into my eyes, and said, "I am always with you. As long as you live in the wisdom I gave you, I am alive, too."

I have found, in the ensuing years of my life, that wisdom like Mama's is a rare and genuine gift. I cherish all that she taught me, and I am conscientious about passing it along to my children, friends, and global family. Throughout history, wisdom has been attributed to the Divine Feminine (Sophia.) Therefore, I accept this gift from Mama as part of my soul contract. I do my very best (again, one of Mama's credos) to add to the wisdom she gave me, and to pass it forward with love. I believe all women who love deeply, and nurture the lives of others, do the same. For as Charles Dickens once said, "A loving heart is the truest wisdom."

. . . .

A busy mother of six, **Kathryn Peters-Brinkley** is the publisher of the acclaimed online publication, Kinetics Magazine: Awakening to Ascension. For over two decades, Kathryn has been at the forefront of the metaphysical/spiritual community as an author, journalist, lecturer, radio talk show host, spiritual wholeness counselor, and wisdom teacher. Kathryn is the author of "Jewels for the Soul: Spiritual Reflections and Affirmations for the Heart and Soul" and co-author with Dannion Brinkley of "Secrets of the Light: Lessons from Heaven." Kathryn also owns and operates a production company with her daughter, Elizabeth. Quantum Multimedia Productions plans and promotes live spiritual conferences and self-empowerment workshops, as well as online teleseminars. www.kineticsmag.com

God's Plan for Our Lives Never Changes

By Tene' Williams, singer and songwriter, best known for the Billboard-topping "Give Him A Love," and president of Sierra Music Group

. . . .

There are no accidents with God. He has a divine plan for each of us – from our beginning to our end – and sometimes His plan is very different from the one we imagined for ourselves. My journey as a woman began as soon as I came to terms with this very salient point.

I grew up in Akron, Ohio, in a home filled with music. My father played bass for the legendary gospel group, the Highway QCs. My mother sang with her family in a local group called the Hewett Singers. My uncle, Howard Hewett, was the lead singer of the hit group, Shalamar. My grandmother had her own television and radio programs and was one of Akron's most prominent concert promoters and political activists. She was known as "the lady with the golden voice." It wasn't long before I realized I, too, had a voice.

As a child, Whitney Houston was my idol. I was enamored of her classy style and pop sound. I copied every one of her moves perfectly. Invariably, after chores, I could be found in front of the TV, watching the newest dance moves and mimicking the artists who appeared on Soul Train. I dreamed that one day I would appear on Soul Train and be interviewed by the great Don Cornelius.

As a teenager, I spent my summers in New York with my dad's family. Somehow, I instinctively knew I would accomplish my dreams there. The summer I was 16, I auditioned for Amateur Night at the Apollo and was chosen to be in the contest. Amazingly, I won three times and was offered a record deal! I also met and began to work with Kyle Bynoe, the man who would become my husband. Together, we created a demo that caught the interest of Mickey Eichner. Unfortunately, I knew I was too young.

"If it's for you, it'll be there after graduation," my mother said. So I went home to finish school.

Shortly after I graduated, my pastor, Dr. Jerome Parker, told me, "You will go into the world and then return." It wasn't what I wanted to hear. Trying to ignore his words, I returned to New York, where Eichner became my manager. He obtained a record deal for me at Elektra's Pendulum Division. The dream I had carried in my spirit since the age of nine – to win the Apollo Amateur Night, to win and perform at the Grammys, and to get the interview with the great Cornelius and sing on Soul Train – was finally coming to fruition.

The early months of 1993 were a pivotal time. Kyle and I had our first child, Kyle Chandler. I also released my first single, "Give Him A Love," and I was set to begin a hectic and demanding promotional tour. Little did I know that everything was about to come to a screeching halt and that I would be faced with some of the hardest decisions of my life, decisions that would alter my life's course dramatically. Although I had done my best to forget my pastor's prediction, his words crept back hauntingly. *You will go out into the world and then return.*

First, my relationship with my manager dissolved. At a time when record companies controlled artists' lives, I committed the ultimate no-no: I got pregnant with my second child. With no manager and the advancement of my pregnancy, I was unable to continue touring. But, I had made my choice.

Gabrielle Sierra made her entrance into the world on July 1, 1995. I had planned to return to the touring circuit four weeks after delivery, just as I had done after my son was born, but you know what they say – want to make God laugh? Make plans!

When Gabrielle was only a few days old, the hospital pediatrician informed us she had a serious heart condition. Before I even had a chance to take her home, I found myself waiting – numb and disoriented – in the office of the local pediatric cardiologist, Dr. Ben-Shachar.

It turned out Gabrielle had a congenital defect called dextrocardia. It meant that her heart, which should have been facing left, was facing right. No one knows what causes dextrocardia, but I couldn't get the word "congenital" out of my mind. With no other explanation available, I began to blame myself. After all, didn't "congenital" mean "while in the womb?"

As if that weren't enough, the doctor also informed us that Gabby had a hole in her heart that would not close on its own. I was besieged by a myriad of emotions. What had I done wrong? What could I have done to prevent this?

At four months old, Gabby had surgery to put a band on one of her heart valves. She came through it like a champ, but we still weren't out of the woods. The hole was still there. We'd only put a Band-Aid over the problem.

At home, I stared at my beautiful blessing from God, held her in my arms, and softly sang to her – all while I racked my brain to determine what I could have possibly done during my pregnancy to cause this. I can't count the nights I cried out to God, begged for my child's healing, pleaded for a miracle. After many sleepless nights, I slowly resolved that my career was officially, and indefinitely, over, and I relinquished the whole situation to God.

After Gabrielle's birth and the dissolution of my relationship with my manager, my husband and I returned to Akron, where we served as part of the praise and worship team at our church, Harvest House Christian Center. There, under the guidance and teaching of our pastors, we grew stronger, and we learned a great conquering strategy: to speak the Word into implacable situations.

We also stopped the pursuit of R&B and Pop music. Instead, I ministered in song on a regular basis. One of my favorite songs to sing was "The Battle is the Lord's." The congregation loved that song, but, most of all, it ministered to me. Even then, I knew the Lord must have a plan I hadn't seen yet, and I decided to trust in Him.

When Gabby was three, we learned she would need to have a critical open-heart procedure, but that she was too small to undergo the procedure safely. If we could delay the surgery until she was five, she would have a much better chance of survival. For two years, my husband and I closely monitored her condition, praying and believing her condition would remain stable until she was old enough to withstand the procedure that would save her life.

God blessed us, and when the time came, we made arrangements for the operation. As we packed for her hospital stay, Gabby told us she wanted a CD player that played CDs "over and over" in her hospital room. We knew she meant one with a continual play function. She also said she wanted two CDs playing in her room at all times. One was a Praise and Worship CD I recorded soon after I returned home from New York. The other was one I do not recall ever having played for her. It was Benny Hinn's, "I Am the Lord That Healeth Thee."

After the surgery, we made sure one of those two CDs played for the duration of her hospital stay. The volume was very low, barely audible, but she, the doctors, and the nurses knew it was there. Gabby rarely needed pain medication, and she was up walking the halls two days after surgery. The doctors and nurses were astounded at how quickly she began to heal. This baby was amazing! She became a living example of how to depend on God.

Almost immediately after surgery, she began her rehabilitation and checkups. She ran and played with her brother and cousins like any other child. For a brief period of time, I almost forgot how serious the condition she faced was.

Even after the first operation, we knew Gabby would require additional surgeries to complete the issues with her heart. When she was ten years old, we were informed it was time. Once again, we cast our cares on God.

By this time, we'd spent almost ten years under the teaching and leadership of our pastors, Drs. Jerome and Barbie Parker, and we had become well versed in the things of God, thanks to their powerful teaching and strong leadership. I understood the Word works when one works the

Word, and I was prepared to be all the woman God called on me to be. Not only that, I was a fierce mother, strong in spirit! We found every Scripture that promised health and recovery and stood on those Scriptures. We would not crumble! We would stand strong in the face of adversity. We knew God wanted us to win!

The doctor said there was no way to know in advance the position of Gabby's heart, to determine if surgery would be successful or if additional surgery would be needed. We prayed for God to reposition Gabby's heart so the hole could be closed completely. We used Scriptures like " . . . the heart of the king is in His hands, and He'll turn it whichever way He desires." Sure enough, when the doctor came to talk with us after the surgery, we could see his smile from way down the hall. Before he uttered a word, we began to thank God for His goodness and mercy. The heart repositioned itself so precisely that they fixed not only that hole, but another smaller one that had been revealed during surgery!

For the second time, Gabby astonished the medical staff with her speedy recovery. Soon she was home and, once again, under the care of Dr. Ben-Shachar. In time, the monthly visits became every two months, then every six months, until finally the doctor saw her annually and only for a checkup. Today, she is a sophomore in high school and has been on the cheerleading squad for three consecutive years. She is a typical teenager who loves hanging out with her girlfriends, dancing, and doing all of the things doctors had previously said she never would do. Besides following in my footsteps as a worshipper, Gabby is a beautiful psalmist. Although God used the doctors, Gabby was miraculously healed.

I now understand my pastor's prophesy of "coming back." I had to return home to build a foundation from which I could know and pursue my true purpose. In 1993, my hit single, "Give Him A Love," stayed on the Billboard charts for an astounding four months. It also remained on the Billboard's recurring chart until 2004, an incredible feat virtually unheard of in the music business. I believe God was holding my place until He was ready to reinstate me in the industry.

Now, I've come full circle, and, frankly, I don't think I've missed a thing! My new single, "Your Love Completes Me," was recently released. Through our company, Sierra Music Group, Kyle and I are a light in the darkness. I know if I had gone another direction, I would not have made it through 19 years of marriage with three beautiful and amazing children: Kyle Chandler, 18; Gabrielle, 16; and Michael, 13. I would not have become an ordained minister, and I would not be writing this story of victory. God took me away from the industry to refine me and restore me. Through my challenges, I have been blessed with a motherly and womanly wisdom.

As women, we graciously can allow our lives to paint a picture of God's love. Everyone is born with a purpose. God has designed a destiny for each of us, and when we walk in that purpose, life becomes simple. With God, all things are possible. To God, and only God, be the glory!

. . . .

The consummate singer and songwriter, **Tene' Williams**, is best known for her hit song, "Give Him a Love," which topped the Billboard charts for four months straight in 1993. Now taking an active hand in her career, the beautiful Tene' is president of her record label, Sierra Music Group. She recently released the CD, "Brave," with the lush, moving ballad "Your Love Completes Me" as the debut single.

Tene' proved her young vocal chops at the world famous Apollo Theater's Amateur Night, winning not once, but three times, wherein she was offered a deal on their Apollo Records. As she was only 16, she decided to complete her education before taking a big professional step. Tene's record label, Sierra Music Group, is distributed by Urban Creed/Universal Music. Tene' loves songs with substance and emotion and is a balladeer in her heart. She wants to bring back the diversity of R&B music, with its strong vocals. Her talent and beauty shine through, more radiant than ever, as she travels her musical road and gifts the listening public with ballads that are embellished by her experiences and filled with her heart. www.tenewilliams.com

I am Wise.

1. I exercise discernment in my choices.

2. I honor the wisdom I possess at every age and stage of my life and through all challenges and all situations.

3. I actively free myself from external noise, allowing my inner wisdom to shine.

4. I make the best decisions I am capable of at the time and allow myself to make different decisions later.

5. I share my wisdom with those who are ready to hear it, and I am gracious with those who are not.

I am Woman

I *shine* my womanly magnificence into the world.

I *embrace* my feminine qualities and focus on how they create goodness in my home and beyond.

I *support, nurture,* and *love* all women and honor their journeys, as I do my own.

I am *collaborative, creative, intuitive, nurturing, strong, wise,* and a *trailblazer.*

I graciously *blossom* into my inherent receptive nature and open myself to receiving the goodness of life.

Ways to Find Balance in the Feminine

Seek to collaborate, but also *lead* with a strong, fair heart.

Embrace your creativity with full abandon, and then allow the intellect to guide its results so that both you and others can fully appreciate it.

Discover a way to distinguish your intuition from your ego.

Appreciate that there is a time to nurture and a time to let go.

Understand that allowing yourself to be vulnerable is part of being strong.

Create your own path in life when needed, but also recognize that some paths already have been blazed for you and that life can be easy and smooth.

Appreciate when your wisdom is best shared, and when it is best saved, and be mindful there is much knowledge beyond that which you are cognitively aware.

Ways to Celebrate Your Feminine

Volunteer with pre-teen and teen girls and help them navigate what can be a sticky time of discovering the feminine nature.

Make it a *priority* to find women who will support you unconditionally, and spend time with them on a regular basis.

Release any guilt you may feel about being "girly," participating in "traditional" roles that feel right to you, and in engaging in feminine activities that nourish your soul, mind, and body.

Allow men to celebrate their masculine.

Create a plan to spend time on a regular basis in a way you find nourishing – and stick to it.

Compliment yourself when you look into a mirror.

Any time you have a negative thought about yourself, "erase" it and replace it with ten *positive* thoughts or compliments.

Appreciate that calm and emotionally wholesome relationships provide opportunities for personal growth.

Exhale, and allow yourself to be *confident* and *secure* in the wisdom of your womanhood.

View food and drink as nourishment for the body, and approach the act of eating as a *sacred part* of adoring and nurturing your physical self.

Exercise in ways that feel comforting and supportive of your *beautiful, womanly body.*

Appreciate that *nature creates,* just as women do, and make efforts to spend more time in it.

Use *supportive* and *respectful* language when discussing other women – and yourself.

Celebrate your body as a temple, and delight in the gift of your sexual nature.

Greet *personal growth* and exploration with childlike openness and eagerness.

Genuinely like yourself.

Appreciate the menstrual cycle as a time for reflection, renewal, and self-nurturance.

Empower yourself during pregnancy and in birth, and trust that your body is a *divine being* of creation with inherent self-knowledge about the process.

Step out of your comfort zone, and then applaud yourself for your *bravery.*

Wear frilly, soft pajamas or undergarments for *your own pleasure.*

Allow yourself to flirt innocently and smile at the world.

Go out of your way to share a supportive comment for another woman's work or mission or daily life.

Decorate your environments in ways that uplift and inspire you to be your *best self.*

Recognize that it is *healthy* to want personal time, and step fully into it.

Read about the feminine nature or any nourishing topic you find appealing, and *share* this information with other women who may be craving the wholeness of their being.

Little Known Ways Women Have Been Saving the World for Centuries

Japan, c. 1000 Muraskai Shikibu writes world's first novel, Genji monogatari (The Tale of Genji.)

Constantinople, 1028 Zoe Porphyrogenita takes the throne as joint ruler of the Byzantine Empire.

Salerno, Italy, 1100 Three new texts on women's health – believed to be written by Trotula of Ruggiero, a female professor of medicine – are released.

Schonau, Germany c. 1161 Elisabeth of Schonau, a Benedictine nun, publishes her widely known visions and the title of "Saint" is added to her name.

Hohenbourg, Alsace c. 1190 Herrad von Landsberg completes her "Hortus Deliciarum" (Garden of Delights,) an illustrated encyclopedia full of biblical, theological, and scientific information.

Assisi, Italy, 1212 Clare of Assisi cofounds Order of Poor Ladies, a new order for religious women.

Poletains, France, 1294 Mystic and prioress of the Carthusian sisters at Poletains, Marguerite d'Oingt publishes "Page of Meditations," which teaches readers how to reach a holy state through the practice of meditation.

Berwick, Scotland, June 10, 1338 Lady Agnes Randolph, Countess of Dunbar (aka "Black Agnes") protects Scotland from English siege.

Naples, Italy, 1414 Giovanna II becomes queen of Naples; she rules for 21 years.

....

Glossary

Collaboration Creativity Intuition Nurturing Strength Trailblazing Wisdom

England c. 1436 Margery Kempe, an uneducated mystic and traveler, publishes the world's first autobiography written in English.

Cadiz, Spain, Sept. 25, 1493 Queen Isabella of Spain sponsors Columbus' second voyage to the New World.

Cambrai, France, Aug. 3, 1529 Louise of Savoy, the Regent of France; Margaret of Austria; and Marguerite, Queen of Navarre negotiate the Treaty of Cambrai, putting an end to the hostilities between France and the Holy Roman Empire.

Brescia, Italy, Nov. 25, 1535 Angela Merici, along with 11 other women, founds the Ursulines, a new religious order that will care for the sick and the needy.

Madrid, Spain, 1559 Italian portrait painter Sofonisba Anguissola becomes the Spanish court portrait painter.

Zazzua, Africa, 1576 Queen Amina leads a military operation to secure safe passage for traders in the region.

Santiago, Chile, 1580 Inés de Suárez, a conquistadora, becomes famous as the only European woman to take part in the military operation to establish Santiago.

Kyoto, Japan, 1603 Izumo no Okuni creates new innovative dance style, kabuki (to shock.)

Jamestown, North America, Dec. 1607 12-year-old Pocahontas saves the life of John Smith.

Paris, France, 1609 Louyse Bourgeois, a royal midwife, publishes the first ever written account of midwifery, "Observations on Sterility."

Maryland, North America, Jan. 1648 Unmarried, Catholic landowner Margaret Brent asks the Assembly of Maryland for the right to vote.

Lancaster, England, 1664 Margaret Fell, a founding member of the Quakers, writes women's rights manifesto, "Women's Speaking Justified, Proved, and Allowed of by the Scriptures."

Newcastle, England, 1666 Margaret Cavendish, the Duchess of Newcastle, publishes world's first science fiction novel, "The Blazing World."

Paris, France, 1686 Françoise d'Aubigné establishes school for the education of impoverished young women.

Montreal, New France (Canada,) October 1692 Marie-Madeleine Jarret de Verchéres, a young girl, holds off a week-long attack on her father's fort with the help of her two brothers and an elderly man.

Neerwinden, Netherlands, July 1693 Kit Cavanagh (aka Mother Ross) fights for William III disguised as a man.

Amsterdam, Netherlands, 1705 Mrs. Maria Sybylla Merian disproves the popular theory that insects arise spontaneously from rotting mud with her groundbreaking science book, "Metamorphosis insectorum surinamensium."

Bologna, Italy, May 1732 Laura Bassi, a brilliant physicist, becomes the first woman to be appointed as a university professor.

Milan, Italy, 1748 Genius mathematician, Maria Gaetana Agnesi, publishes a groundbreaking book that simplifies differential calculus and other math ideas.

Halle, Germany, June 13, 1754 Dorothea Christiane Erxleben becomes first female ever to receive medical degree.

Newport, Rhode Island, Aug. 22, 1762 Ann Smith Franklin becomes the first female editor in North America.

Dublin, Ireland, Sept. 1827 Catherine McAuley opens House of Mercy, a new Catholic school for destitute women and orphans.

New York, USA, 1872 Victoria Woodhall, first female U.S. stock-broker, receives the Equal Rights Party's nomination for President.

Stockholm, Sweden, 1905 Pacifist and writer, Baroness Bertha von Suttner, becomes first woman ever to receive a Nobel Peace Prize.

Rome, Italy, 1907 Dr. Maria Montessori opens Casa dei Bambini, the first of what later became known as the Montessori schools.

Epsom, England, 1913 Emily Davison steps in front of a running horse at the Epsom Derby in order to gain publicity for the suffragette cause.

About Absolute Love Publishing

Absolute Love Publishing is an independent book publishing house founded on spiritual principles. Our mission is to create and publish projects that promote goodness in the world.

We have published internationally-renowned and Billboard-topping musicians, Olympic athletes, prominent media professionals and authors, inspirational and visionary figures, innovative change-makers, spiritual leaders, and more. Absolute Love Publishing is located in Austin, Texas, USA. It owns min-e-book.com and the trademark, min-e-book™. A min-e-book™ is a shorter-style e-book designed for a quick read.

Absolute Love Publishing is also home to the imprint Spirited Press, an assisted self-publishing platform that assists writers with a la carte book editing, marketing, and publishing services.

www.AbsoluteLovePublishing.com
www.min-e-book.com
www.SpiritedPress.com

About Caroline A. Shearer

Caroline A. Shearer is the founder of Absolute Love Publishing, which was born out of a mission to create and publish projects promoting goodness in the world. Known as a fresh, distinctive, spiritual voice, Caroline's visionary leadership is uplifting, gently blending love and inspiration. She is regularly featured as a luminary in print, broadcast, and online media; where she offers guidance and shares positive stories of her personal spiritual journey toward a more abundant, joyful, and light-filled life. Intuitively guided, Caroline has a remarkable ability to unite others along a path of progressing and celebrating the experience of humanity.

A bestselling author, Caroline's popular books include, "Dead End Date," the first book in the Adventures of a Lightworker metaphysical mystery series; "Love Like God: Embracing Unconditional Love;" "Love Like God Companion;" "Raise Your Vibration: Tips and Tools for a High-Frequency Life," a min-e-book™, and "Women Will Save the World." In addition to her own projects, she recently founded Spirited Press, an assisted self-publishing imprint that operates under the umbrella of Absolute Love Publishing. Spirited Press supports authors in sharing their own messages with the world.

Other Books by Absolute Love Publishing

Adventures of a Lightworker: Dead End Date

"Dead End Date" is the first book in a metaphysical series about a woman's crusade to teach the world about love, one mystery and personal hang-up at a time. In a Bridget Jones meets New Age-style, "Dead End Date" introduces readers to Faith, a young woman whose dating disasters and personal angst have separated her from the reason she's on Earth. When she receives the shocking news that she is a lightworker and has one year to fulfill her life purpose, Faith embarks on her mission with zeal, tackling problems big and small – including the death of her blind date. Working with angels and psychic abilities and even the murder victim himself, Faith dives headfirst into a personal journey that will transform all those around her and, eventually, all those around the world.

Love Like God: Embracing Unconditional Love

In this groundbreaking compilation, well-known individuals from across the globe share stories of how they learned to release the conditions that block absolute love. Along with the insights of bestselling author Caroline A. Shearer, readers will be reminded of their natural state of love and will begin to envision a world without fear or judgement or pain. Along with Shearer's reflections and affirmations, experts, musicians, authors, professional athletes, and others shed light on the universal experiences of journeying the path of unconditional love.

Love Like God Companion Book

You've read the love-expanding essays from the luminaries of "Love Like God." Now, take your love steps further with the "Love Like God Companion Book." The Companion provides a positive, actionable pathway into a state of absolute love, enabling readers to further open their hearts at a pace that matches their experiences. This book features an expanded introduction, the Thoughts and Affirmations from "Love Like God," plus all new "Love in Action Steps."

**"Raise Your Vibration: Tips and Tools for a High-Frequency Life,"
a min-e-book™**

Presenting mind-opening concepts and tips, "Raise Your Vibration: Tips and Tools for a High-Frequency Life," a min-e-book™, opens the doorway to your highest and greatest good! This min-e-book™ demonstrates how every thought and every action affect our level of attraction, enabling us to attain what we truly want in life. Divided into categories of mind, body, and spirit/ soul, readers will learn practical steps they can immediately put into practice to resonate at a higher vibration and further evolve their souls. A must-read primer for a higher existence! Are you ready for a high-frequency life?

All Books Available at www.AbsoluteLovePublishing.com.

Printed in Great Britain
by Amazon.co.uk, Ltd.,
Marston Gate.